*George Washington
and the Two-Term Precedent*

George Washington and the Two-Term Precedent

David A. Yalof

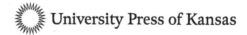 University Press of Kansas

Published by the University Press of Kansas (Lawrence, Kansas 66045), which
was organized by the Kansas Board of Regents and is operated and funded by
Emporia State University, Fort Hays State University, Kansas State University,
Pittsburg State University, the University of Kansas, and Wichita State
University.

Library of Congress Cataloging-in-Publication Data

Names: Yalof, David Alistair, author.
Title: George Washington and the two-term precedent / David A. Yalof.
Description: Lawrence, Kansas : University Press of Kansas, 2023. | Series:
    Landmark presidential decisions | Includes bibliographical references
    and index.
Identifiers: LCCN 2022054876 (print)
    LCCN 2022054877 (ebook)
    ISBN 9780700635948 (cloth)
    ISBN 9780700635108 (paperback)
    ISBN 9780700635115 (ebook)
Subjects: LCSH: Washington, George, 1732–1799—Influence. |
    Presidents—Term of office—United States. | United States. Constitution.
    22nd Amendment. | Executive power—United States—History. |
    Roosevelt, Franklin D. (Franklin Delano), 1882–1945. | Presidents—United
    States—Decision making. | United States—Politics and government.
Classification: LCC E312 .Y35 2023 (print) | LCC E312 (ebook) | DDC
    973.4/1092—dc23/eng/20221116
LC record available at https://lccn.loc.gov/2022054876.
LC ebook record available at https://lccn.loc.gov/2022054877.

British Library Cataloguing-in-Publication Data is available.

Printed in the United States of America

10 9 8 7 6 5 4 3 2 1

The paper used in this publication is acid free and meets the minimum
requirements of the American National Standard for Permanence of Paper for
Printed Library Materials Z39.48–1992.

To Andrea, Rachel, Jane, and Benjamin

CONTENTS

FOREWORD

Studies of the American presidency are typically stories of elections won, power wielded, and legislation enacted. Political scientists judge presidents by their political skills, their eloquence and vision, their power to persuade, and their organizational capacity and decision-making styles. Presidents are measured by what they accomplish with the power bestowed upon them by the American people and the Constitution. The nation's greatest presidents are those we associate with great and lasting achievements, such as the end of slavery and the defeat of Nazi Germany.

However, the nation's first president, George Washington, staked his claim to greatness not only on what he did with power but on his willingness to give it up—indeed his insistence that he give it up. Washington was revered by his contemporaries as much or more for resigning his command of the Revolutionary armies at the close of the war as for the military battles he won against the British. The countless eulogies that poured forth upon Washington's death in 1799 invariably singled out for praise this act of self-denial, which set him apart from history's many triumphant generals who could not resist the allure of the dictator's powers.

Washington's record of restraint extended to the presidency when he stepped down at the close of his second term to return to private life. Back then, there was no two-term tradition, let alone a Twenty-second Amendment requiring that he give up power after two terms. His popularity was still sky-high, and a third term would have been his for the asking. Advisers and supporters urged him to run again, telling him that he was the indispensable one without whom the young republic might not survive. Yet Washington chose once more not to hold on to power but to relinquish it.

How Washington made this decision, and its significance for American democracy, is the subject of David Yalof's penetrating study. In deciding not to stand for reelection in 1796, Washington did not envision a strict two-term limit that would bind all his successors. However, he was keenly aware that as the first president his actions would set precedents that would inevitably shape the behavior of future incumbents. To stay in office until his death would have lent credence to the anti-Federalist charge that the presidency was little better than an "elective monarchy." Washington's great refusal, Yalof shows, was in part a way of modeling for Americans "the free and peaceful transfer of power to a new president." That we have generally taken the peaceful transfer of power for granted in the United States is in no small part a tribute to the force of Washington's example.

Yalof's book could hardly be more timely, arriving as it does on the heels of President Donald Trump's extraordinary efforts to remain in power even after losing a free and fair election in 2020. As Yalof reminds us, Trump not only tried to cling to power after defeat but suggested that he deserved a third term to make up for Democrats' efforts to spoil his first one and even praised a Chinese constitutional amendment that removed presidential term limits, enabling the "great" President Xi Jinping to be "president for life." Lest any in the audience miss his meaning, Trump added: "Look, he was able to do that. I think it's great. Maybe we'll have to give that a shot someday."

Whether the country is better served by the Twenty-second Amendment is, of course, up for debate. Partisan polarization and the reduced power of incumbent presidents to frame the national discourse arguably mean there is less need for the Twenty-second Amendment than in the twentieth century and that we can therefore trust in democratic elections alone to ensure a healthy rotation in the nation's highest office. On the other side of the ledger, the powers of the presidency are vast and growing, and elections, even when they are not subverted, are crude instruments of popular control.

Whatever one's view of the Twenty-second Amendment, there is no denying the significance of what Yalof calls Washington's "parting gift to the nation"—the decision to voluntarily depart from the nation's highest office. It is a gift that has kept on giving to American democracy. But Trump is a reminder that Washington's gift is as precarious as it is precious. Its ultimate power rests not in laws or even the Constitution but in the civic virtue of the nation's citizens and leaders. Among the great virtues of Yalof's compelling history is that it helps us to recognize that restraint in the pursuit and exercise of power lies at the heart of Washington's claim to greatness. That lesson, like this excellent book, is one that every American should ponder.

Richard J. Ellis
Willamette University

PREFACE AND ACKNOWLEDGMENTS

Even in our current, hyper-polarized political era, there is at least one issue that citizens from all ends of the political spectrum can still agree upon: The office of President of the United States has become perhaps the most difficult job in the world.[1] In representing more than 300 million diverse citizens, this one official must act as commander-in-chief, legislator-in-chief, head of state, and so much more—all from the confines of a transparent bubble where he or she undergoes the most intense public scrutiny in the world on a daily basis. Given all this, on those rare occasions when an individual proves even modestly successful at the job, it would seem only logical to allow that person to remain in office for as long as possible . . . assuming (of course) that the electorate agrees. And yet our current system of government makes that impossible, denying even the most popular and successful presidents the opportunity to successfully run for more than two terms in office.

Frustrations with the term limits imposed on American presidents both by our political culture and, since 1951, by constitutional amendment are shared by supporters and officeholders alike. Consider some modern presidents' very public musings on the topic:

- Late in his second term, Ronald Reagan vowed during a television interview that he wished to start a movement that would repeal the Twenty-second Amendment's prohibition against a president running for a third term in office.[2]
- Early in 2000, Bill Clinton told *Rolling Stone* that he wanted to run for a third term even as his second term had been marred by the holding of an impeachment trial and numerous scandals.[3]
- On a 2020 episode of *The Late Show with Stephen Colbert*, Barack Obama informed the host that he missed the "fascinating work" of the presidency; the former president even playfully suggested that he would be willing to serve a third term through a front man with an earpiece, as he delivered lines for his stand-in from behind the scenes.[4]

Indeed, the prospect of Obama's return has become something of a running joke in popular culture: in the 2017 movie *Get Out*, one character offered his willingness to vote for Obama yet again as clear proof that he could not actually be considered racist.

All three of those chief executives finished their second terms with approval ratings that were sizeable, at least by recent standards.[5] And yet none were able to go before the voters to seek a third term as president, even if they wanted to. For that, they can blame not just the Twenty-second Amendment, but the man whose example made such a legal barrier to additional terms unnecessary for the first 151 years of the nation's history: George Washington. No Gallup polls existed when Washington departed the presidency in March of 1797, but safe to say, no one has ever left the presidency more esteemed in the eyes of the public. Buttressed by his larger-than-life reputation, Washington won his first two presidential elections by acclamation, and by all accounts, he would have won a third straight election as well with little effort on his part. Even those who mercilessly attacked Washington's policies during his second term as president acknowledged that practically speaking, the job was his for as long as he wanted it.

Still, Washington walked away. As a result, many questions about that third term were never answered. If Washington had stayed, would he have been able to maintain American neutrality in the ongoing hostilities between Britain and France, especially after French privateers began attacking merchant ships in American waters? Would American efforts to negotiate long-term peace with French officials have gone better under his leadership? Would Washington have been able to stave off Congressional passage of the controversial Alien and Sedition Acts of 1798? And would the "Father of his Country" have been able to keep the government funded exclusively by excise taxes and tariffs, avoiding the extremely unpopular Direct Tax Act passed by Congress in July of 1798? Because George Washington walked away after two terms, we will never know how his third term would have turned out, or whether it would have changed our perceptions of him going forward.

As president, Washington was no doubt concerned about all these ongoing issues for the newly-created nation. Yet his larger concern was with the nature of presidential power in a democratic republic. Though aware of the need for a strong chief executive, he did not want to create a virtual monarchy that would invite abuse. In short, Washington clearly hoped to influence the decisions of his successors: he did not want them overstaying their welcome as head of the executive branch. In this respect, he was mostly successful: until Franklin Roosevelt secured a third term in 1940, presidents were exceedingly reluctant to challenge Washington's two-term precedent. Moreover, the bare handful that did so were quickly rebuffed by their parties, the public or both. Since 1951, the Twenty-second Amendment has served as an even more formidable obstacle to a third term. But it was Washington who got there first.

As I write these words, the United States is undergoing a seismic reexamination of its heroes and how they are celebrated in the twenty-first century. Monuments to Confederate war generals like Robert E. Lee and slave-owning founding fathers like Thomas Jefferson have been removed from the public square; their names have been eradicated from public buildings in northern and southern states alike, including New York, Louisiana, North Carolina, and Texas. The New York City Public Design Commission offered no apologies when it voted unanimously to remove a statue of Thomas Jefferson from its City Hall in October of 2021. And yet George Washington, who was a slaveowner himself, has mostly escaped such scrutiny. How does he manage to maintain such a firm hold on our polity? Other than perhaps his celebrated crossing of the Delaware river—an event which occurred nearly seven years before the American Revolutionary War even ended—there are few iconic moments or events that serve to symbolize or encapsulate the scope of his contributions. Certainly none of his writings or speeches ever came close to making history or capturing the public's imagination the way Jefferson's Declaration of Independence or Thomas Paine's *Common Sense* clearly did.

Rather, Washington's hold on our political system arises primarily from the reputation he cultivated as a leader who quietly and unobtrusively put the needs of the nation above everything else. Washington accomplished that first as a general, when he kept his beleaguered Continental Army on the field for eight long years, steering it away from devastating defeats even as it teetered on the edge of collapse. He did so once again as a political figure without a formal office in 1787, when he lent his quiet support to the holding of a constitutional convention in Philadelphia, and then presided over that convention without making any speeches or otherwise revealing his sympathies. As president, Washington's most notable accomplishments came in the form of evasion: he avoided a war with Britain that he knew could not be won, and he kept partisan warfare at bay during the nation's earliest years by providing a place for leaders of both factions to air their views within his administration. George Washington was not one to offer grandiose demonstrations of victory. In this respect, there is no more fitting testament to his life and service than the Washington Monument itself: Other than the Latin words *Laus Deo* (which translate to "Praise be to God") found on an aluminum cap atop the memorial, it features no memorable quotes or inscriptions of any kind. The Washington Monument thus appropriately represents the man whom historian Joseph Ellis describes as the most "fully concealed" of the founding fathers.[6] It would be left to others to inject his life with significance.

Washington's professional career as a general and politician was filled with examples of understated service to the public. And yet his most significant act of all came at the very end of his presidency, when he refused to stand for a third term as president. This book focuses on that singular act, which might be the most important decision any US president has ever rendered in the pursuit of democratic government.

Washington's decision to walk away from a near-certain election victory in 1796—and with no assurances as to who his successor might be—was as striking to citizens at the time as it still appears to us today. In 1787, members of the political elite watched as Washington returned from private life to preside over the constitutional convention, and then the following year, to stand for election as the nation's first president. Once he was persuaded to run for a second term in 1792, the act of running yet again in 1796 seemed almost inevitable. Alexander Hamilton and Thomas Jefferson had appealed to his patriotism in pressing the case for his reelection in 1792—they both believed Washington was the only figure who could effectively manage the various factions that had emerged in US politics. Those same forces that kept him in office beyond 1792 had not dissipated by late 1796, as his second term was nearing its conclusion. If anything, partisanship had grown even more divisive over the previous four years, threatening to unravel the young nation. The Federalists (led by Hamilton) focused on the commercial sector of the country, while Jeffersonian Democratic-Republicans drew their strength from farmers and agrarian interests. Though the Jay Treaty supported by Washington had helped avert war with Great Britain, it had angered France and bitterly divided Americans. The federal government had been forced to put down the 1794 Whiskey Rebellion, in which farmers on the western frontier had risen up to protest taxes applying to all distilled spirits.[7] Given all these events, how could Washington possibly resist running again?

The list of political leaders who have voluntarily relinquished significant political power when they had the chance to maintain it without a fight is not long. Among US presidents, James Polk pledged to serve just one term when he was first elected in 1844, and he voluntarily departed on schedule four years later. Theodore Roosevelt made a pledge not to run again when he secured a presidential election victory in his own right in 1904, and he honored that pledge in 1908. (He ran unsuccessfully as a third-party candidate in 1912.) Other presidents (such as Andrew Jackson and James Monroe) walked away from likely third-term victories at least in part out of deference to Washington's example. It is impossible to know whether their decisions would have been different had Washington died in office, rather than leaving voluntarily.

Looking beyond the United States for such examples, Nelson Mandela stands out for having voluntarily stepped down after just one term as South Africa's president in 1999. For better examples, one might go much farther back to ancient Rome. Diocletian, who ruled over Rome from 284 through 305 A.D., abdicated his emperorship voluntarily even though he was still immensely popular and viewed as indispensable to maintaining stability throughout the empire. And of course there was Lucius Quinctius Cincinnatus, who became a legendary figure precisely because he resigned in 459 B.C. from a position of near absolute authority in the Roman republic. That we must go back so far in history to find these iconic examples tells us all we need to know about the meaning and significance of George Washington's decision.

To be sure, George Washington saw nothing especially meaningful in serving exactly two terms or eight years.[8] What mattered more to him

was that he departed the presidency voluntarily and peacefully; he was
not forced out by an election defeat or even by the realistic possibility
of such a defeat. Nor did he wish to die in office. The so-called two-
term precedent became the dominant narrative of Washington's departure only because so many of his successors—starting with Thomas
Jefferson and ending with Harry S. Truman—essentially repeated the
gesture. For Washington, it was the nature and circumstances of the departure that offered his greatest contribution to the polity.

Writing in 2018, John Dickerson ventured his opinion that Washington would never recognize the office of the presidency today, though
he would certainly sympathize with its modern occupants who face the
same challenge he did of fulfilling impossibly high expectations.[9] Washington's determination that he not overstep the boundaries of the office
and create a monarchial presidency established a political culture that
binds modern presidents today, many of whom—if anything—seem too
small for the office they occupy. Perhaps Washington knew exactly what
he was doing when he walked away from the presidency in March of
1797. At a minimum, we should fully explore that possibility.

Several people directly assisted me in the preparation of this manuscript, and my undying gratitude to them won't come close to evening
the score. Andrea Pierce Yalof (my spouse of over three decades) carefully read the manuscript from beginning to end on multiple occasions.
She contributed thoughtful criticisms and advice for improving nearly
every part of this manuscript. John Dabrowski was endlessly patient in
responding to my requests for research help. Both Michael Nelson, the
editor of this Landmark Presidential Decisions series, and David Cong-
don of the University Press of Kansas were encouraging throughout
this process and offered helpful suggestions at the outset that kept my
eyes squarely on the ball. I cannot thank them enough. Dr. Stephen H.
Browne of Penn State University, a fine scholar of George Washington in
his own right, provided important and useful observations that helped
me strike the difficult balance between providing well-grounded history
on one hand, while at the same time utilizing accessible prose. Dr. Richard E. Ellis of the University of Buffalo went through the manuscript in
painstaking fashion and provided helpful feedback as well, especially

with regard to how I engaged with the work of other scholars. The manuscript is in a far better place thanks to their constructive suggestions.

Among the many others to whom I owe a personal thanks are Patrick Schmidt, a close friend, with whom I continue to share all the joys and frustrations of being a professor; Larry Bowman, whose friendship has been a lifeline for me since I first arrived in Storrs twenty-five years ago; Susan Herbst, who always keeps me grounded and focused on the things that really matter; Vin Moscardelli and Virginia Hettinger, who can still make me laugh out loud after nearly three decades of friendship; Oksan Bayulgen, whose hospitality and friendship know no bounds; Jane and Lewis Gordon, who enjoy authentic Chinese food almost as much as I do; Brian Waddell, a fellow New York Mets fan who has been a frequent travel companion and confidante; and of course, all my other friends and colleagues at the University of Connecticut, including (but hardly limited to) Sam Best, Jeffrey Dudas, Frank Griggs, Shareen Hertel, Kristin Kelly, Jeffrey Ladewig, Yoni Morse, Dave Richards, and Jeremy Pressman. Jeremy in particular has challenged me again and again to justify my positions; he has forced me to defend them and improve them along the way.

Of course, my family's encouragement and support help make this (and everything else I do) possible. Andrea, Rachel, Jane and Ben . . . what would I do without you? I may truly be the luckiest man on the planet.

November 2022
Storrs, Connecticut

Introduction

George Washington
and the Two-Term Precedent

*"The orderly transfer of authority as called for in the
Constitution routinely takes place, as it has for almost
two centuries, and few of us stop to think how unique we
really are. In the eyes of many in the world, this every
four-year ceremony we accept as normal is nothing less
than a miracle."*

Ronald Reagan, January 20, 1981

The peaceful transfer of power from one political faction to another—
once considered the bedrock of the US political system—was tested like
never before on January 6, 2021. The events of that afternoon—in which
a violent mob tried to disrupt Congress's certification of Electoral College votes from the 2020 presidential election—offered Americans a so-
bering reminder of just how fragile a democracy can be. Until that day,
most Americans had taken electoral transitions for granted, and with
good reason: no attempt to overturn an election by violent means had
occurred in the 232 years following ratification of the US Constitution.[1]
To put this in perspective, a recent study of elections around the world
found that during that same period, sixty-eight countries had *never once
experienced a peaceful transition of power.*[2] How exactly did the United
States endure so many seamless transitions from one political leader to
another with nary an incident until 2021?

As with so many other features of our political system, our understanding of this process must begin with George Washington. The man
credited with winning the American Revolutionary War, presiding over
the 1787 constitutional convention, and then serving as the nation's first
president made perhaps his greatest contribution of all when he essentially routinized the peaceful transition of power from the outset.

By walking away from the presidency in 1797, Washington took that

1

first critical step in making the peaceful transition of power a core American tenet. Because the first US president remained overwhelmingly popular at the end of his second term, he could have retained the office without much effort. Instead, Washington voluntarily relinquished his position as chief executive and offered his blessing to a successor (John Adams) whom he had rarely consulted during his presidency. In handing over that power so effortlessly and with no strings attached, the first peaceful transition of power occurred without a hitch under a new and untested Constitution. One might dismiss what Washington accomplished in this regard as the case of a tired president following the rules he had played a part in establishing. But it was far more than that: George Washington transformed an episode so often characterized by serious disruptions (if not outright violence) around the world into an uneventful process.

As a testament to the event's underlying importance, Washington delayed his departure from the Capitol in Philadelphia just long enough so he could appear at Adams's inauguration ceremony at the House of Representatives' chamber in Congress Hall on March 4, 1797. Those present that day understood the moment's significance, if only because Washington was the only chief executive that the nation had ever known. Indeed, because Washington had served as commanding general of the Continental Army, *he was the only real leader the nation had ever known.* Wearing a plain black suit, Washington arrived at the event shortly before Adams. The outgoing president received clamorous applause: the ovation for him was louder and more sustained than that which was given minutes later to the new president or the newly elected vice president, Thomas Jefferson.[3] No one questioned these would be difficult shoes for anyone to fill.[4]

When Adams rose to give his address, he stood close to the spot where he himself had nominated Washington to serve as commander-in-chief of the Continental Army back in June of 1775.[5] Understandably, the new president felt compelled to address his predecessor's departure early in his speech, using clear and unambiguous terms. Remarking on Washington's decision to return home to Mount Vernon, Adams conceded that the president had not just paved the way for his own personal ascension, but he had laid a foundation for the success of the greater

American experiment as well. According to the new president, in that retirement which is his *voluntary choice*, may he long live to enjoy the delicious recollection of his services, the gratitude of mankind, the happy fruits of them to himself and the world, which are daily increasing, and that splendid prospect of the future fortunes of this country which is opening from year to year . . . [6]

For Adams, it was the voluntary nature of the departure that was the critical takeaway, as it both glorified Washington's act while at the same time relieving his successor of any undeserved blame for prematurely forcing Washington out of office. Privately, Adams believed Washington might well have stayed but for his frustrations with the partisan warfare being waged by Hamilton and other cabinet members.[7] In terms of public consumption, the new president planned to leave no doubt that Washington freely chose to set the peaceful transition of power into motion.

Immediately following the speech, Washington congratulated Adams, and then exited the ceremony quickly.[8] This was his second critical step in helping to execute a peaceful transition, as he wished to leave no question of his refusal to somehow maintain power behind the scenes. Washington had no intention of undermining the legacy he had worked so hard to cultivate of a leader who was willing to voluntarily surrender power.

The First American Icon

George Washington departed the US capital as an immensely popular demigod who represented the values of self-sacrifice and duty in the minds of an adoring public.[9] In truth, this image of selflessness helped to mask the reality that Washington was by all measures an extremely ambitious politician.

As a young man from a wealthy Virginia family, Washington desperately sought higher status and an exalted place within the planter aristocracy of Virginia. He was not a "true-born" gentleman, as he did not receive the formal education in England that was made available to his older brothers. He first became a land surveyor, but determined early on that the most certain path to advancement in society would come through successful military service, and so he worked hard to secure a promotion to lieutenant colonel of a Virginia regiment under British command during the French and Indian War. Fierce ambition continued to drive him as he sought progressively higher military positions, culminating in his being named commander-in-chief of the Continental Army in 1775. Washington also amassed significant wealth by his marriage in 1759 to Martha Dandridge, who brought to their formal union a significant estate gained from her first marriage to Daniel Parke Custis, a rich planter who died in 1757.[10]

Thus began a pattern that extended throughout Washington's lifetime. At that time in America, to be viewed as anxious for power was "simply not done."[11] The future president took this need to foreswear such aspirations to a new extreme: he had great difficulty acknowledging such ambition to anyone, concealing it behind an image of disinterestedness or apathy. Later in life, his repeated invocation of the call to public duty aligned both with what he wanted to believe about himself, and with what others wanted to believe about him. The first test of this image occurred at the end of the war for independence. Unlike Julius Caesar, Oliver Cromwell, and so many other military leaders who had translated their military triumphs into grants of even greater power by staying in their current positions, Washington stepped down as commander of his Continental Army in 1783 at the height of his glory and power. He did so proactively, before critics could accuse him of lusting for power.[12] That he did so willingly and eagerly only added to his public reputation as a man who put the nation first and his own interests second.[13]

Ambitions aside, Washington was reluctant to take on a position in the new US government after the war. What could he possibly do but tarnish his larger-than-life image? Eventually, though, he was driven back into the spotlight by his continued frustration with the Articles of Confederation. The Confederation Congress had been unable to offer him support for soldiers during the war, and he remained frustrated with the ineffectual government under the Articles as a civilian as well.[14] For years he had called for constitutional reform; finally, in 1787, he agreed to preside over the constitutional convention in Philadelphia as a mostly silent participant. It was only a matter of time before he would be drafted by acclamation to serve as the first president under this new constitution.

Washington was determined that his presidential reign be brief—he never ruled out stepping down even before completing his initial four-year term. Unfortunately, this plan to leave after such a short stint as president proved no match for the forces that would press his presidency to continue. The most brilliant official in the capital, Secretary of the Treasury Alexander Hamilton, was Washington's closest ally and protégé. Hamilton frequently fought with other cabinet members, and he had created more enemies than friends, making a presidential run of his own exceedingly unlikely.[15] For him, keeping George Washington in office as long as possible was the highest priority. The same went initially for Secretary of State Thomas Jefferson and Congressman James Madison. Though they disagreed strongly with many of the president's more nationalist policies, they believed his commitment to neutrality would prevent the United States from siding with Great Britain in a war against France.[16]

Washington became indispensable in the minds of many, and he faced no actual opposition in his first two presidential election contests. By all accounts, he would have met only limited opposition had he sought a third term as well.[17] The decision to depart the presidency in 1796 was thus the culmination of a deep internal struggle pitting what he viewed as his personal interests against the continued call of duty to public service. It offered a skeptical world its first real sign that the American experiment would not "degenerate into disorder."[18] It was the decision that is most closely tied to Washington's legacy even today. And it remains one of the most important decisions in the history of the American presidency.

George Washington and the Making of Non-Judicial Precedent

Judicial precedents and the principle of *stare decisis*—the legal doctrine that obligates courts to follow earlier judicial decisions when ruling in a similar case—have long been the backbone of our judicial system and the rule of law. Because the American legal system depends so heavily on unwritten common law created by judges, prior rulings or judgments of courts establish precedents by which subsequent judges within the same court system must normally abide. Of course, *stare decisis* is by no means absolute: all courts recognize the occasional need to correct erroneous decisions or modify decisions based on changed circumstances. And it remains notoriously difficult to predict when courts will actually do so. The US Supreme Court, for example, has explicitly overruled more than two hundred of its own decisions over the years. And there is no coherent or stable conception of precedent that allows us to predict when the Supreme Court (or any court for that matter) will rely on *stare decisis* and when it will depart from it.

A comprehensive look at Washington's decision to forego a third term in office forces us to examine a related phenomenon: that of *non-judicial precedents*. Equally important but less well understood, non-judicial precedents most often arise from decisions reached and actions taken by the system's political actors: governors, mayors, and other executive branch officials throughout federal, state, and local government; legislatures, councils and boards at every level of government; and of course, from all the political actors in the federal government, including the president of the United States.

Some non-judicial precedents are established by formal written opinions. State attorneys general and the US attorney general issue official legal opinions in their capacity as legal advisors to executive officials in their respective governments. While these opinions constitute official statements of an executive officer, they are technically just advisory statements and are not mandatory orders in any traditional sense. Still, absent clear legal guidelines to the contrary, their opinions enjoy the force of law. A recent example arose when President Donald Trump fired Attorney General William Sessions in November 2018 and appointed Sessions' chief of staff, Matthew Whitaker, to serve as acting attorney general without seeking Senate approval. The state of Maryland and nine other entities filed suit to stop the appointment, claiming that Whitaker's appointment violated the Constitutional requirement of Senate confirmation. In response, the Department of Justice's Office of Legal Counsel issued a twenty-page opinion justifying the appointment. The DOJ's formal written opinion did not technically resolve the issue once and for all, but it laid down a clear instruction that filled a void in the guidelines. Future administrations might well consult that opinion if they were to face similar scenarios going forward.

Far more often, political actors seek to establish non-judicial precedents in the form of informal norms or customs they choose to follow. These types of precedents are rarely written down and are usually acknowledged only as the conduct of routine business or processes. And yet the meaning or value they hold may be significant, depending on how many officials follow the norm and whether they publicly acknowledge that norm along the way. In the absence of a formal hearing or event that produces a definitive written or recorded statement of the non-judicial precedent being adopted, subsequent authorities may have "great latitude to choosing" which of them, if any, to rely on for "similar or analogous events."[19]

Non-judicial precedents based on unwritten norms may arise from relatively rare events in the American political system like the impeachment of a sitting president or the circumstances of wartime. Legislatures and executives alike may be reluctant to bind successors in such fact-specific circumstances. Still, they may also arise in the form of more regular practices or traditions. For example, presidents from Thomas Jefferson through William Howard Taft delivered their state-of-the-union addresses to Congress by letter. Woodrow Wilson bucked that non-judicial precedent by delivering the address in person, a practice that was followed by most subsequent presidents.[20]

During his presidency, Washington was determined to shape his office by establishing non-judicial precedents that would guide his successors under most circumstances. On one hand, he understood that one of the central goals of the constitutional convention was to establish a presidency powerful enough to play an influential role in domestic and foreign affairs. Thus, from the beginning of his presidency, Washington modeled an active vision of the chief executive in government. Yet he was equally determined that the presidency not be abused—that it remain accountable to the other branches and the political system as a whole. All his actions helped establish non-judicial precedents that might restrain future presidents. This book focuses primarily on the decision to depart after two terms in office. His determination to leave when he did (and the justification he offered in doing so) stand out among all these non-judicial precedents.

Cultivating the Two-Term Precedent

Consider how the two-term precedent impacted the twenty-nine presidents who served between George Washington's departure in 1797 and Franklin D. Roosevelt's ascension to the presidency in 1933. Washington's example did not just influence the seven presidents who served exactly two terms during that span (Jefferson, Madison, Monroe, Jackson, Grant, Cleveland and Wilson). It also influenced two more presidents (Theodore Roosevelt and Calvin Coolidge) who served significant portions of two presidential terms before leaving the White House of their own accord.

Between 1796 and 1932, nine chief executives served all or part of two separate terms as president and then faced the decision of whether or not to run for yet another term. That select list includes two presidents who joined Washington in being memorialized on Mount Rushmore (Jefferson and Theodore Roosevelt); the founding father most responsible for shaping our Constitution (James Madison); a president who won two of the most lopsided presidential contests in history (James Monroe); the founder of the modern political party system (Andrew Jackson); and the former general who led the union to victory in the Civil War (Grant). Joining them on the list are Grover Cleveland, Woodrow Wilson, and Calvin Coolidge.

It is a simple but telling reality that prior to FDR, *not one of those nine presidents came close to threatening Washington's unwritten two-term precedent.* As noted above, Washington never defined his departure specifically in those terms, and several of the nine chief executives identified above could have argued that Washington's example was not even applicable to their own circumstances. Perhaps the man who came closest to securing a third term as president was Theodore Roosevelt, who completed the term of William McKinley before successfully winning the White House in his own right in 1904. Still, when Theodore Roosevelt sought the presidency once again in 1912, he was arguably not defying Washington's precedent (at least by one interpretation of his actions) because he was only actively seeking the presidency for a second time. Moreover, did Washington's example counsel against serving a third term in office, or serving a third *consecutive* term in office? In 1799, Washington personally rejected early calls that he come out of retirement and run again for president in 1800. Still, had he lived past December of 1799, it is impossible to know how Washington would have reacted to a last-minute draft of his candidacy by Federalists desperate to keep power out of Thomas Jefferson's hands.

The true significance of the two-term precedent may also be demonstrated by an even more amazing fact: *Not one of those nine presidents even managed to secure his party's nomination to run for a third term as president.* Of the nine, only Theodore Roosevelt would ever again compete in a general election, and he did so only as leader of the short-lived Progressive ("Bull Moose") Party after Republicans rejected his bid to replace President William Howard Taft at the top of the ticket in 1912. Ulysses Grant failed to win the nomination at the Republican Party's 1880 convention despite holding a lead on early ballots among the delegates. And Woodrow Wilson's long-shot bid to stay in office in 1920 was viewed as a dead letter among the Democratic Party bosses who had watched Wilson sidelined by illness for much of the previous year. One might reasonably expect that most presidents (especially those who are still in office) would enjoy a decided advantage in seeking their party's nomination for a third term, if only because they offer experience in the office (and as a candidate) that others in the party simply cannot match. Yet even with that advantage, two-term presidents in the nineteenth and early twentieth centuries proved unable to secure their party's nomination for another term.

In 1940, Franklin Delano Roosevelt successfully secured an unprecedented third term as president under extreme circumstances, as World War II was slowly threatening to drag in the United States as a full-fledged combatant. Even so, another term for FDR was never a certainty. As we learn in Chapter 3, FDR knew better than anyone that his confrontation with history would be fraught with complications.

Wrestling with a Precedent Like No Other

George Washington's decision to abandon efforts at reelection in 1796 has become one of the most monumental and significant decisions in American history. It exerted an influence over subsequent US presidents far beyond what the decisionmaker himself ever could have imagined. It made third-term bids by even the most successful presidents extremely unlikely. It also established a rhythm in presidential politics that has shaped the political system, for better or worse. Since Thomas Jefferson's presidency, second-term chief executives have been treated almost as lame ducks from the outset: whatever honeymoon they hoped for disappears quickly into the ether, as politicians from both political parties begin to navigate the political world beyond them. Presidential hopefuls from the incumbent's own party freely launch their own discreet (and not-so-discreet) campaigns for their party's next presidential nomination without regard to whether those efforts might undermine the current president's plans. Meanwhile, the opposition party, anticipating an "open election" for the White House, watches hopefully as the cyclical nature of American politics swings back into their favor. This rhythm of presidential politics was in place long before the Constitution was amended to prohibit full third terms. Had Washington's example not shifted the presumption against a potential third term, the incumbent would likely have remained the focus of speculation throughout his second and subsequent terms. The ratification of the Twenty-second Amendment put those questions to rest after 1951, but Washington established the tradition that gave rise to that amendment more than a century and a half earlier.

One of George Washington's greatest fears was that by dying in office, he would create a precedent for future presidents to serve for life, with impeachment and conviction for high crimes and misdemeanors the sole means of forcing rotation in office. This was not such a far-fetched idea. In the late eighteenth century, even the heads of countries with forms of democratic accountability could direct all the levers of government to maximize their chances for reelection. Three months after the close of the constitutional convention, Jefferson wrote a letter to Madison in which he commented on this very danger:

Experience concurs with reason in concluding that the first
magistrate will always be re-elected if the Constitution permits
it. He is then an officer for life. . . . Reflect on all the instances in
history antient [sp] and modern, of elective monarchies, and say if
they do not give foundation for my fears, the Roman emperors, the
popes, while they were of any importance, the German emperors till
they became hereditary in practice, the kings of Poland, the Deys of
the Ottoman dependencies . . . the only way to prevent disorder is
to render them uninteresting by frequent changes. An incapacity to
be elected a second time would have the only effective preventative.
*The power of removing him every fourth year by the vote of the people is
a power which will not be exercised.*[21]

Jefferson was a witness to ineffectual elections that had undermined
budding democracies. He wrote to Madison of the current King of Poland, Stanislaw August Poniatowski, who was first elected king by the
Polish Diet in September 1764. The Diet retained the absolute power to
remove him, but despite numerous crises, it could never actually do so.

By stepping down voluntarily, Washington injected a measure of
democratic accountability into this new polity by creating a cultural
foundation built on the natural rotation of officeholders. He established
a model for chief executives serving a limited number of terms, with the
prospect of re-election holding them accountable and less susceptible to
corrupt or ill motives. Jefferson's willingness to hold to Washington's example—followed in turn by Madison and Monroe—transformed Washington's decision into a precedent that took on immense significance.

In this contribution to the University Press of Kansas's Landmark
Presidential Decisions Series, I consider George Washington's momentous decision to return home voluntarily after two terms in office
from several different angles and perspectives. Leo Tolstoy warned us
against the folly of satirizing normative history to make it seem recog-
nizable only through the biographies of great leaders. For the great
Russian writer, doing so was analogous to believing that the hands of
one's watch resting at ten o'clock causes the neighboring church bells to
ring. The causes of historical events are infinitely varied and forever un-

knowable, and so historical writing that claims to explain the past may necessarily falsify it. As we wrestle with the precedent first established by Washington, we should keep in mind the degree to which we tend to read history backwards to find the precedent, when the evolution of that custom may have in fact developed nonetheless in unanticipated or unintended ways.

Hindsight is not always 20/20; what seems inevitable to us now can be the result of a series of unlikely and improbable events. This danger can arise in nearly all forms of historical interpretation, but it is even more likely when we confront the mythology surrounding a man whose face sits atop Mount Rushmore and every dollar bill, and who is honored every day by having the U.S. capital (and a central monument in that capital) named after him. While the founding fathers fell hopelessly short by twenty-first-century standards in their treatment of African-Americans, women, Native Americans, and other minority groups, so too do they appear overly prescient and forward-thinking in their creation of constitutional government. The press and commentators of the times in which they lived were far more capable of scrutinizing George Washington and his colleagues precisely because they were not so clouded by the knowledge of how things eventually turned out.

This work seeks to assess events as they unfolded in the 1780s and 1790s, before they were framed in our current, all-knowing historical perspective. What George Washington believed he was doing in 1789, 1792, and 1796 is relevant to this analysis precisely because he was an imperfect predictor of how events would evolve over the next two decades, much less over the next 230 years of American history. What hopes and dreams did he hold for the young republic at the outset? Did he imagine what alternate paths were likely if subsequent leaders ignored his example? This type of analysis may lead us to some unexpected places, at least up until 1951, when the newly ratified Twenty-second Amendment ended the hopes of two-term presidents seeking to extend their tenures as president.

In Chapter 1, I first address the constitutional origins of the chief executive: what did the founders intend for the president in terms of both tenure and accountability? At the constitutional convention in Philadelphia, delegates considered the length of the new chief executive's term in office, and his eligibility to run for reelection. Advocates of eliminating eligibility for reelection focused on the disincentives of a one-term president. Would impeachment and removal prove true to the task of rooting out corruption in the executive branch? The chapter then turns to George Washington's background and motives when he ran for president first in 1788–1789 and then again in 1792. What was Washington's actual understanding when he agreed to serve as the nation's first president, and how did that understanding evolve as partisanship and the two-party system took shape in the early 1790s? Why did he decide to run for reelection the first time? Given Washington's commitment to utilizing a strong cabinet to promote his policies, how did two of those cabinet members (Jefferson and Hamilton) influence him and his views on the nature of the presidency?

Chapter 2 then turns our attention to George Washington's second term and the events leading up to his decision not to seek a third term in office. As president, Washington navigated the federal government through numerous challenges. The image that was first shaped during the spring and summer of 1796 when Washington reached his momentous decision to leave the presidency (and then defended it in his Farewell Address) is the image burnished in the public's mind even today. In weighing concerns that he was becoming too powerful a figure in American politics, the establishment of precedent becomes a factor to some degree in the president's thinking.

Chapter 3 then addresses the aftermath of Washington's decision to return to Mount Vernon after his refusal to stand for reelection in 1796. In building on the events of his second term, the chapter assesses the legacy Washington actually left the country when he voluntarily stepped down from power. The chapter also considers George Washington's successors as a way of understanding the significance of the two-term precedent. The narrative of nineteenth- and early- twentieth-century presidents wrestling with the implications of Washington's example receives extended attention. How much of a barrier to three terms did George Washington actually create? Two presidents linked by strong partisan ties (Jefferson and Madison) could step down knowing that their successors (Madison and later Monroe) would carry their ideological torches and perhaps expand (rather than subvert) their presidential legacies. FDR's four straight election victories followed by ratification of the Twenty-second Amendment are only the final pieces of the puzzle. They did not occur in a vacuum; they were necessarily reacting to the history that came before them.

Finally, in the conclusion we seek to assess the legacy of George Washington's decision. The two-term precedent was not the only factor in these presidents' decisions to depart the White House and not seek a third term as president, but it cast a shadow over many successive presidents' deliberations. A fair and honest analysis of George Washington's precedent and its impact must take into account the ways that non-judicial precedents appear to carry extra weight when history simply follows that precedent. The so-called "Great Man" theory of history espoused by the Scottish philosopher and essayist Thomas Carlyle[22] gives too much credit to a great figure in his influence over others. As long as subsequent presidents and their supporters were forced to wrestle with the precedent, that offers some evidence of its non-binding influence on the political culture, if not on the individuals forced to navigate through it.

CHAPTER 1

Sacrifice (1787–1792)

The Quest for a Limited Executive

"As the first of everything in our situation will serve to establish a precedent, it is devoutly wished on my part that these precedents be fixed on true principles."

George Washington, in a letter to
James Madison, May 5, 1789

The Journey West . . . and Back

The journey from his home in Mount Vernon, Virginia, to the backwoods of Western Pennsylvania must have seemed unbearably long to George Washington and the men who accompanied him when he traveled there in September of 1784: one hundred and fifty miles north along dirt roads to reach Philadelphia, and then another five hundred miles over thirty-four days to rural Ohio County. This was not a trip Washington had ever wanted to take in the first place, but it would have an impact on him that was profound and lasting.

When the war for independence concluded with the signing of the Treaty of Paris in 1783, Washington had defied Loyalist predictions that a military leader as powerful as him would never voluntarily relinquish his command. On multiple occasions during the war, General Washington had declared his intention to resign at the earliest possible opportunity once American independence was assured; yet when that moment came and he actually carried through on his promise, it still came as a surprise to many.[1] As far away as London, subjects of the British crown marveled over Washington's willingness to voluntarily give up power. King George himself reportedly told aides that if Washington performed such an iconic act, he would become "the greatest man in the world."[2] At the same time, Washington's closest aides were hardly surprised at all. After eight years of battle, the general was thoroughly exhausted. To his friend Marquis de Lafayette, Washington declared, "I am retiring within myself." These words suggest a man who at that time possessed "a bone-deep exhaustion of body . . . but also of mind and perhaps of spirit as well."[3]

Shortly after he formally resigned from the army, Washington returned to life as a country squire on the same Mount Vernon plantation his family had owned since 1674. At the time, he had no intention of ever returning to public life.[4] Instead, he sought intellectually stimulating dialogue from friends and other sources outside the government. Notably, he agreed to serve as president-general of the newly formed Society of the Cincinnati, an organization created "to promote knowledge and appreciation of the achievement of American independence." Washington was well aware of the symbolism he was thereby embracing: his first postwar act was to head an organization named after the Roman patrician who became a legendary figure of civic virtue by stepping down from power and returning to his farm.

To be sure, Mount Vernon offered anything but a quiet life, as scores of visitors arrived at the Washingtons' estate starting in early 1784 to discuss politics. Before the war, neighbors, friends, and business associates throughout Virginia had dropped by Mount Vernon frequently, and the Washingtons had welcomed overnight guests more than half the days of the year in the late 1760s.[5] After the revolution, however, the list of guests expanded to include foreign dignitaries visiting from Europe. Mount Vernon had become an essential stop on any such visit to the American states.

From these visits, Washington and his wife learned firsthand that the newly independent nation was struggling. Washington had always regarded the Articles of Confederation as "woefully inadequate to meet the needs of a dynamic growing country."[6] Now the evidence for that position was mounting. Of greatest concern was the monetary debt crisis which had exploded after the war. Drained of its resources, the US government had failed to deliver to veterans of both the Continental Army and state militias their promised bounties, land grants, and other forms of reimbursement for their service. European economic interests were frustrated as well. Foreign merchants insisted that the Americans pay for goods with hard currency; they refused to extend lines of credit to American customers, including rural farmers who suddenly found themselves unable to meet their obligations.[7] Meanwhile, Britain, France, and Spain closed ports in the British West Indies and elsewhere to products not carried on their own ships, and American manufacturers struggled to compete. Under the Articles of Confederation, Congress had little power to enact navigation laws. All this contributed to significant political unrest. Elites (including Washington) suffered financially as states in economic turmoil were unable to engage in any form of cooperative commerce or economic development initiatives on their behalf.

Settlement in the West carried its own set of additional problems. Land speculators who had acquired vast tracts of land found themselves in frequent conflict with settlers. Who would settle these disagreements? Over a decade earlier, Washington had discovered that his estate actually owned 1,644 acres of backwoods in an area of Pennsylvania west of the Alleghenies, which was now known as Perryopolis. It was a gift from the Colony of Virginia in consideration of his service during the French and Indian War. Hearing of the growing chaos out West, Washington was determined to visit his Western properties during the fall of 1784. Once so comfortable that he had agreed to serve as a general of the Continental Army without pay,[8] the Mount Vernon estate had now fallen on hard times. The Washingtons had been forced to amass large debts just to keep the estate up and running during the revolution.[9] Now these debts were coming due, and the Washingtons' failure to collect many years of rent in arrears left them in significant financial hardship. Stated simply, Washington needed his Western properties to bring him and his family badly needed revenue.[10]

George Washington had never before visited the land in question. When he finally reached Perryopolis after nearly forty days of travel, he found that a mill on the property had run dry thanks to the failings of a local mill operator.[11] Still, a mill could be fixed; a more thorny problem arose in the form of "Seceders"—Scottish Presbyterians who believed they had purchased the land Washington now claimed from Colonel George Croghan, a former deputy Indian agent for the British and fur trader who had been banished from the frontier in 1777. Led by David

Reed, the Seceders had settled the land in the 1770s by building fences and log cabins on the property while Washington was away at war. The former general was determined to at least enforce his legal rights to back rent.

When efforts to settle with the Seceders failed, Washington knew he faced an uphill battle to clear the title. The law in Pennsylvania at that time was relatively clear: "There was a general presumption that settlers who improved land had priority over an absentee landlord with only a paper title."[12] And yet if he accepted the Seceders' claim, squatters throughout the backcountry of Pennsylvania would be emboldened to claim the rest of his land as well. Moreover, it was not just his own land claims at stake, but those of many others who would follow him on this "Potomac Route to the West" in subsequent years. To clear the title once and for all, Washington was going to have to sue. And he would need a national government steeped in legitimacy and authority if he hoped to gain any real support for his claims.

At the trial to settle the claims two years later, Pennsylvania Supreme Court Justice Thomas McKean found that the former general had legitimate title to the land and awarded Washington a complete victory on the merits. Right after the verdict, Washington softened his stance somewhat by relenting on his demand for back rent as way of making peace in his absence. Washington maintained control over the land for another decade until 1796, when he sold the land to a local agent for $12,000.

The Perryopolis episode had a profound impact on Washington's thinking. His conception of a legitimate government extended further than just an entity that settled land disputes; a government must be able to enforce laws and exercise authority over matters, even in the absence of legal proceedings. Events like these were not lost on other elites throughout the territories: If the mythic George Washington was forced to struggle so mightily just to retain land rights he rightfully and lawfully owned, what chance did others have going forward? Would the laws of the governments established along the eastern seaboard of this new nation even be respected in the frontiers of the new west? These were no longer foreign enemies waging battle against Washington: the Seceders epitomized the common man, and they had dutifully cleared the forest, put up fences, and built cabins. Everyone knew the deeds

Washington and his aristocratic class held were often flawed. And yet if those deeds could simply be wiped away by what amounted to technical errors, legally sound claims to the western lands would not be worth the paper they were written on.

Even before he was forced to wage a land fight in Western Pennsylvania, Washington had made his position clear on the need for a new constitution. Months after the Treaty of Paris, he sent a letter to all the state governments arguing that the six-year-old Articles of Confederation—the same articles that had made it so difficult to fight the war—were like a "rope of sand" linking the states only nominally. Among his many criticisms of this arrangement was the lack of any effective executive branch—it was just "an endless multiplicity of committees" which were "wretchedly managed."[13]

The Articles of Confederation crippled the new nation's economic standing in numerous ways—the federal government struggled to regulate trade with foreign countries and was unable to retaliate when other countries imposed unfair restrictions on American goods. While states imposed duties on neighboring states, the federal government stood by powerless. To Washington, "only a stronger, more effective national government could bring America back from the 'brink of precipice' and save it from plunging into ruin."[14]

After returning from the trip out west, Washington spoke to numerous friends about the necessity of a stronger union. To Governor Edmund Randolph of Virginia, he argued that if nothing else, the object of such a union must be "to connect the Western territory with the Atlantic states."[15] The following year, he agreed to become president of the Potomac Company, an entity jointly chartered by Virginia and Maryland to construct a much desired water route linking the states to the West.[16] More than anyone, Washington understood the importance of projects in which multiple state governments cooperated to encourage commerce among different regions.

Two years later, when delegates from just five states met in Annapolis in 1786, Washington was not yet ready to lend his authority to revise the Articles of Confederation. By contrast, the Philadelphia convention held the following summer would offer him the opportunity to create an executive branch worth fighting for.

The Quest for an Effective Executive
under the Constitution

By 1787, Washington was committed to the need for a constitutional
convention that would dramatically modify the Articles. That did not
mean he was free of concerns about the impact his participation in Philadelphia could have on his reputation. Nor was he reassured by the
general consensus among the delegates in Philadelphia that he would
likely become the first president of a reconceived United States government.[17] The former general was plainly worried that any actions he took
in furtherance of these developments would open him up to charges of
"inconsistency" and "ambition," given that just four years earlier, he had
pledged to never again meddle in public matters.[18] Washington's sensi-
tivity about his reputation made it difficult for him to decide what to do
as he "puzzled out the effect different steps might have on his standing
with the people."[19] But in this case, the stakes were simply too high:
standing on the sidelines in Mount Vernon while the newly independent
alliance of American states descended into chaos was no longer an op-
tion for the fifty-five-year-old Washington.

He thus arrived in Philadelphia ready to advocate for certain guiding
principles. Among them was his preference for provisions that strength-
ened the executive branch by ensuring the chief executive was a single
individual not chosen or appointed by the legislature; and that the executive had veto power over laws, which could in turn be overridden by
a significant majority of the Congress.[20] Cognizant of how it would appear if Washington was seen to be advocating for provisions that vested
himself with power, he agreed to preside over the convention (and thus
lend his authority to its everyday proceedings) while maintaining outward silence on the merits of all individual proposals. In this way, Washington stood as the "personification of nationalism at the constitutional
convention," while still voicing his opinions at dinner with small groups
of delegates behind the scenes.[21]

The question of how to construct a more effective executive branch
was discussed at length during the earliest stages of the 1787 constitutional convention. Delegates in Philadelphia debated issues concerning
the necessary qualifications of the executive and the powers delegated

to and withheld from the office.[22] On the question of presidential terms, they considered two interconnected questions about the nature of executive service: (1) What would be the most appropriate length for an executive term? and (2) Would the executive be eligible to run for reelection? When the delegates took up these latter two questions during the first week of June, they understood that the answers they reached would apply first to George Washington, who was certain to be chosen the first president of the United States by acclamation.

The various state governments differed widely in their approach to these questions. Out of the twelve states that sent delegates to Philadelphia, exactly six included gubernatorial term limits of some form in their state constitutions, with Delaware requiring that its governor leave after a single three-year term. Five other states featured one-year terms for their governors: after three consecutive terms, they were ineligible to run again for three or four years.[23] Meanwhile, the remaining six other state constitutions included no term limits whatsoever, although the prominence of legislative election as the mechanism for choosing executives (found in two-thirds of the states) served as a check against governors using their position to turn reelection contests into processes of routine approval.

Surprisingly, the delegates reached an early consensus that presidents should be elected (presumably by Congress) to a single seven-year term, with no eligibility to run again. The so-called Virginia and New Jersey plans were "virtually indistinguishable" on this point.[24] Washington's old friend Edmund Randolph, the chief sponsor of the Virginia Plan, knew his audience favored a lengthy term with no eligibility to continue. Accordingly, he placed this proposal before the delegates during the last week of May in 1787. Within these limits, the executive would have the "general authority to execute the national law," along with all those executive powers granted to him under the Articles of Confederation Congress. Advocates of the "small states plan" (or "New Jersey plan") did nothing to counter Randolph's views on this issue. When William Paterson of New Jersey presented his own plan to the delegates sixteen days later, he maintained indifference as to the length of years in the presidential term, though he too agreed with making the president ineligible for a subsequent term.[25]

Though James Madison had dutifully drafted the Virginia plan in line with the views of the Virginia (and Pennsylvania) delegations as a whole, he was never in lockstep with Randolph or Paterson on the benefits of term limits. To Madison, undue power did not derive from continued service, but from a lack of accountability. Thus, he believed the mere possibility of additional terms was unlikely to invite executive tyranny . . . if anything, an executive with no incentive for reelection would pose a greater danger as an unchecked political entity. The better way to check executive wrongdoing would be through the impeachment process; Madison believed that mechanism should be the central method for preventing a man "from holding office longer than he ought."[26]

Though badly outnumbered at the outset, Madison had an important ally in his opposition to term limits: Gouverneur Morris, the superintendent of finance of the United States, who was now serving at the convention as a delegate from Pennsylvania. Like Madison, Morris worried that by removing the possibility of another term, the new Constitution "would destroy the great motive to good behavior, the hope of being rewarded by reappointment."[27] Morris further suggested that term limits would potentially invite corruption: "It will tempt [the president] to make the most of the short space of time allotted him to accumulate wealth and provide for his friends."[28] Morris thus openly advocated for a shorter term with eligibility to run again.[29]

A handful of other delegates had been arguing for much longer terms. Elbridge Gerry of Massachusetts, for example, favored ten-, fifteen-, or even twenty-year terms for the chief executive.[30] And Alexander Hamilton proposed a "permanent president" who would serve for life or during good behavior.[31] His position was based on his undying faith in the British model, which sought to place executives beyond temptation: "[A]n executive is less dangerous to the liberties of the people when in office during life."[32] Hamilton stood nearly alone in this regard, with few other delegates joining his cause. Yet along with Morris and Madison, Hamilton's speeches played a role in reframing the debate in the direction of achieving a truly independent executive who would not be subject to legislative dominance. By July 26, 1787, most of the convention delegates still held to Randolph's original formulation: "legislative selection, a seven-year term, and ineligibility for reelection."[33] However, enough questions had been raised that the delegates agreed to revisit the issue several weeks later.

As the convention neared its conclusion in late summer, a series of dramatic events led to a reconsideration of the Madison/Morris position on term limits. On August 31, 1787, the delegates appointed and charged a newly formed "Committee on Postponed Parts,"[34] consisting of exactly one member from every state other than New York, with settling such tabled issues and parts of committee reports that had not yet been acted upon. In order to facilitate debates and keep the convention moving forward, the delegates had previously postponed deciding several crucially important matters including (1) the mechanism for selecting a president and (2) the length of a presidential term and eligibility for reelection. Now this new committee chaired by David Brearly, chief justice of New Jersey's Supreme Court, would play a key role in deciding the debate over presidential terms. First, the committee adopted the Electoral College Plan as a means of selecting presidents.[35] This permanent abandonment of legislative selection of a president effectively shifted the mood of the committee (and eventually the convention as a whole) against a seven-year term with no eligibility to run again. According to the political scientist Thomas Cronin, it was as if, with the establishment of the Electoral College, "the controversy surrounding the four-year term seemed almost suddenly to have disappeared."[36] It helped that Madison and Morris were well positioned as members of this new committee to capitalize on the shift. That committee essentially devised a compromise based on the Madison/Morris position in a matter of days: the seven-year term was shortened to four years, with term limits removed altogether.[37]

On September 6, 1787, the committee approved the new Electoral College mechanism and the new provisions for four-year presidential terms by a 10-1 vote. Outside the committee, many powerful individuals were angered by the decision to eliminate term limits altogether. Delegates George Mason and Elbridge Gerry were especially outspoken in their opposition, as were other important figures outside of the convention, including James Monroe and former Virginia governor Patrick Henry.[38] None of this resistance derailed the committee's influence on the final outcome, however: its recommendations became a part of the final constitution draft, which received thirty-nine signatures on September 17, 1787.[39]

As the debate over executive terms was being waged that summer in Philadelphia, where was George Washington? True to his word, the presiding officer of the convention remained publicly silent on these and other issues. Friends and acquaintances understood that the revolution had left him committed to a few core principles that he would urge on the new government. Government should be close to the people. States' interests must give way to the greater good of the nation. And when it came to the executive branch, he believed in a single strong executive that was not dependent upon (and certainly not to be elected by) the legislature.[40] Yet he did not press any of those views on the convention floor. According to Robert F. Jones, his contribution to the success of the convention was "not in the work of drafting a new Constitution . . . [i]t lay in his simply being there."[41]

That does not mean he held no private views on the specific question of whether presidents should be ineligible for subsequent terms. In a letter penned to Marquis de Lafayette in early 1788, Washington rejected the premise that ineligibility for reelection would help guard against corruption, as

> [t]here cannot, in my judgment, be the least danger that the
> President will by any practicable intrigue ever be able to continue
> himself one moment in office, much less perpetuate himself in it—
> but in the last stage of corrupted morals and political depravity . . .[42]

By 1787, Washington had come to believe that some kind of ruling elite might well be necessary if the new republic were to survive its early period as a country. And he was equally certain (based on his own experiences) that members of that same ruling class would be less likely to drag out their time in office as a means of accumulating personal riches. For all his eloquence about humility and his invocation of Cincinnatus, Washington's return to private life in 1783 had been driven in part by a fear that his home estate might soon default on its loans. It seemed to Washington that one term in office—whether four years or more in length—would be more than enough for an aristocrat like himself. Term limits would not be necessary to check corruption under those circumstances.

George Washington dutifully signed the Constitution along with thirty-eight of the fifty-five delegates who attended sessions of the convention. Before leaving Philadelphia, Washington sent copies of the brand-new document both to Thomas Jefferson and his fellow commander in the war, Marquis de Lafayette. Washington also lent his imprimatur to the proceedings by sending a copy to fellow residents of his home state who were believed to be the most active opponents at the constitution, including Patrick Henry.

Though he was not an author of the eighty-five articles and essays that would later be known as "the Federalist Papers," Washington would become an active proponent of ratification behind the scenes, urging friends of the Constitution to take up their pens and answer the critics.[43] When James Madison revealed to the former general that he was in fact one of the Federalist Papers' anonymous writers, Washington passed on draft copies of the essays to a friend and politician, David Stuart, so they could be more widely disseminated throughout the colonies.[44] Washington specifically praised Hamilton for his contributions to the Federalist Papers, telling him that he had "read every performance which has been printed on one side or another of the great question."[45] That included Federalist No. 72, in which Hamilton had forcefully argued that term limits for the chief executive would have "diminish[ed] inducements to good behavior" by freeing the executive of accountability.[46]

For state legislators who remained on the fence about ratification, Washington clearly lent a significant amount of prestige to this cause. And yet Washington kept a decidedly low public profile, coordinating the campaign strictly through private correspondence while otherwise maintaining a "very evident public silence."[47] Knowing that his presence might well turn the tide in a state that was closely divided on ratification, he nevertheless stayed away from the Virginia ratifying convention in Richmond. His reasons for doing so were personal more than strategic. Did Washington really believe his influence would be stronger if he maintained a detached image? More likely, he was already thinking about his reputation and legacy if he was elected president. As such, he did not want to appear as if he had lobbied for the ratifications of a constitutional government that would afford him even more power than he already had, because he was not interested in gaining more power. For him, the acceptance of that presidential office was never about power . . . only duty.[48] Even in his private reflections, Washington voiced support for the Constitution, but nothing but "hesitancy and lamentation about the burden shortly to descend on him."[49]

There was also the matter of Washington's long-time relationships with anti-federalists in Virginia who were adamantly opposed to ratification. Many of them warned of unbridled executive authority under the Constitution. To avoid offending George Washington and his supporters, the "Federal Farmer" (a pseudonym for an anti-federalist writer) published pieces that attempted to sidestep any such criticism of the former general:

> Give a man such power and his greatest objective will be to keep it . . . this will be the case with nine-tenths of the presidents . . . we may have for the first president a great and good man, governed by superior motives; but these are not events to be calculated upon in the present state of human nature.[50]

Not all opponents of ratification would be so kind, including some of his closest friends. Patrick Henry, for example, remained noncommittal in the weeks leading up to the Richmond convention, but in truth he was a lost cause on the issue of ratification. Henry opposed the Constitution for the exact same reason that his friend Washington had supported it: it created a strong executive. The battle to free Virginia from King George of England simply could not culminate in the surrendering of those powers to yet another potential tyrant. Thus, Henry deemed the Constitution "a backwards step," and a betrayal of those who had died in the Revolutionary cause.[51] Consistent to the end, Henry would later turn down George Washington's offer to become secretary of state in an administration whose federalist leanings contradicted his own political philosophy.

Washington wisely believed he would have more success courting Randolph, who had actually played a leading role in Philadelphia. Randolph was one of just three convention members who left after refusing to sign the final document; unlike Henry, his concern was not so much with executive power as it was with the other branches of government. He thought that the federal judiciary would pose a threat to state courts, and he considered the Senate too powerful and Congress's overall power far too broad. Though never formally identified as an anti-federalist, Randolph did publicly distribute an account of his objections to the document in October 1787.[52] For practical reasons, Randolph eventually flipped once again at the Virginia ratifying convention, where he urged the Constitution's approval, arguing that "it was too late to attempt to amend it without endangering the Union." (Eventually Randolph would accept Washington's offer to become the nation's first attorney general, and then later its second secretary of state). The battle for ratification forced Washington's final break with older revolutionaries like George Mason and Patrick Henry in favor of the younger generation of leaders such as James Madison.[53]

Washington stayed in contact with Madison throughout the Virginia ratifying convention and was gratified to learn that on June 25, 1788, his home state became the tenth to ratify the Constitution, if only by a narrow 89–79 vote. Virginia's vote was not technically necessary as the document had become binding four days earlier, when New Hampshire became the ninth state to ratify. Yet Virginia carried outsized importance in the process as the new nation's most populous state. The commonwealth also included some potentially key contributors to the new union, including Madison, Randolph, and Jefferson. Would Washington participate in the new government if his home state cast its lot in opposition? From the perspectives of Madison and Hamilton, that was a prospect they could not stand to ponder.

The First President of the United States

Washington faced no actual opposition during the first quadrennial election of an American president. Even so, much of what happened between formal ratification of the Constitution in June 1788 and the conclusion of that first election in January of 1789 provides us with important clues as to Washington's interests and motivations.

George Washington did not anticipate the bitter partisanship among supporters of the Constitution that would divide the country during its initial decade; yet looking past ratification, he was concerned about persistent divisions between federalist and anti-federalists that he had seen firsthand in his home state, and which had nearly derailed a positive vote at the Virginia ratifying convention. What might unite these factions and prevent the anti-federalists from undermining the new government? So many of his old friends had opposed this new entity, including many who had watched him resign his military command voluntarily and declare that he was departing public life. Would they now support Washington after he had so quickly broken his promise to exit public life?

Despite Washington's fears of being accused of breaking his vow, honor might also flow the opposite way, compelling George Washington to accept the presidency out of principle. One historian posited the question in this way: "How could [Washington] lead the fight to dismantle one government without risking failure at the helm of the new?"[54] Given all his efforts to establish a new constitutional government, the former general now considered the possibility that it was his "duty" to accept the presidency. Perhaps he needed to believe that because it would be impossible otherwise to abandon Mount Vernon once again. To a man focused on how his every move would be viewed by the public, duty also offered an important justification for taking on the risks to his reputation. Washington understood quite well that "it would be a miracle" if he were to leave office as esteemed as when he went in.

If Washington still harbored doubts about taking on the presidency after all this personal deliberation, his closest advisors were ready to put the issue to rest. Always the strategist, Alexander Hamilton appealed to Washington's understanding of how international relations actually worked. He wrote a letter to his mentor in which he argued that "the point of light in which you stand at home and abroad will make an infinite difference in the respectability in which the government will begin its operations in the alternative of your being or not being the head of state."[55] Washington knew that he offered a degree of legitimacy to the new government, and on that single point he needed little persuasion. Another challenge soon presented itself: to prevent anti-federalists from undermining the new government from within. When Washington learned that opponents of the Constitution were pressing the name of New York Governor George Clinton as president or (far more likely) as vice president, Washington uncharacteristically waded into the fight, announcing that he considered John Adams better suited to the position. Yet as Willard Sterne Randall fairly asks, "How could he choose the vice president if he were not willing to become president?"[56]

Once Washington's candidacy was a certainty, there remained the question of how to properly conduct the election during this upcoming period. If the process appeared to be a mere coronation of Washington, it would validate the concerns of anti-federalists who opposed ratification out of fear that the Constitution was creating a form of monarchy. Thus, in the leadup to his formal election by acclamation, local versions of these parties campaigned for Washington as a means of increasing turnout in those states where popular votes would determine which electors were chosen. Washington set the tone by steering clear of any maneuvers that might fuel charges that he planned to rule as a monarch. Without political parties, he was under no pressure to endorse candidates for the Senate or the House, and he refused to do so. To keep the still-fragile union stitched together, all the founding fathers (including Washington) favored a vice president who hailed from a northern state. Numerous pro-ratification politicians fit the bill, including John Adams, John Hancock, and Benjamin Lincoln of Massachusetts; Samuel Huntington of Connecticut; and John Jay of New York. When the Electoral College finally met, all sixty-nine electors cast one of their two electoral votes for Washington. John Adams appeared on thirty-four of the sixty-nine ballots and was thus the runaway choice for the vice presidency—the remaining thirty-five votes were spread among ten different candidates. Finally, New York City was slated to be the seat of government at the outset, until a more permanent location took its place.

Congress hoped to certify Washington's election by March of 1789, but due to bad roads, it could not muster the quorum it needed until April. Twenty-nine days prior to assuming the presidency on April 30, 1789, Washington penned a letter to Henry Knox, his close friend and the former chief artillery officer of the Continental Army, who had agreed to serve as the first secretary of war in his new administration. In what historian James Flexner later called one of the darkest letters Washington ever wrote, he summed up his extreme reluctance to serve, while at the same time articulating how he felt the need to push those concerns aside due to the precarious future the United States was now facing:

> in confidence I can assure you—with the world it would obtain little credit—that my movements to the chair of Government will be accompanied with feelings not unlike those of a culprit who is going to the place of his execution: so unwilling am I, in the evening of a life nearly consumed in public cares to quit a peaceful abode for an Ocean of difficulties, without that competency of political skill— abilities (& inclination) which is necessary to manage the helm—I am sensible, that I am embarking the voice of my Countrymen and a good name of my own, on this voyage, but what returns will be made for them—Heaven alone can foretell.[57]

In another letter to his friend Edward Rutledge, Washington continued with the theme of execution, arguing that in accepting the office, he had given up "all expectations of private happiness in this world."[58]

Nor did Martha Washington offer much encouragement to her husband. When Washington set out from Mount Vernon on his journey to New York on April 16, 1789, she "watched her husband of 30 years depart with a mixture of bittersweet sensations."[59] Martha had long doubted the wisdom of this final act in his public life and thought it too late for the fifty-seven-year-old to serve in public life once again. But like her husband, she knew it could not be avoided, especially once the presidency was couched in terms of his serving a greater duty to the republic. Indeed, as Washington would later explain: " at my time of life and in my circumstances, nothing but a conviction of duty could have induced me to depart from my resolution of remaining in retirement."[60]

To Washington, "the establishment of our new government . . . the last great experiment for promoting human happiness" fit clearly within the scope of that duty.[61]

At his first inauguration held on April 30, 1789, on the balcony of Federal Hall in New York City, President Washington made clear as he took the oath of office that his presence at that moment represented a decision to choose the travails of public service over the "allure of private content."[62] George Washington knew better than anyone that no other office would bear so heavily on the character of its occupant. Both Washingtons hoped his presidency would amount to a short stint lasting no more than a single term, if that long. This was wishful thinking on their parts. Yet Washington never wavered from that assumption, even after the reality of his election as the nation's first president began to hit home.

The First Term

As president, George Washington's policies and actions spoke to his greater intent to pursue two critical goals. First there was the desire to establish a strong and powerful executive whose absence from the Articles of Confederation had been one of several critical flaws spurring the constitutional convention to life in the first place. As deeply as he believed anything, "Washington was certain that national impotence must cease. . . . He meant to persuade both his compatriots and European statesmen that 'we act for ourselves and not for others.'"[63] Simultaneously, Washington had a second goal: he hoped to assure citizens—especially anti-federalists and others who opposed ratification of the new Constitution—that this newly emboldened presidency would *not* become an all-powerful monarchy. He was determined to model an executive strong enough to be effective, but duly checked by the other branches and the polity as a whole. By establishing a strong chief executive, he would help ensure the legitimacy of this new Constitution.

In pursuit of an emboldened presidency, Washington took several critical steps during his first term in office: (1) he established an English-style cabinet system with secretaries in charge of key departments meeting in a forum for exchanging ideas and considering proposals for submitting major legislation to Congress; (2) he dispelled worries over who would command the US army by assuming the role of singular military leader; (3) he kept the vice president at arm's length, imposing a mostly ceremonial role on the executive branch's second-highest officer; (4) in addition to six new Supreme Court Justices, he appointed a successor to chief justice from outside the bench; (5) he helped select a more permanent site for the US capital along the Potomac river; (6) he ensured that the collection of tariffs and import duties would provide the new government with a permanent source of funding; and (7) he sought to enforce US sovereignty in western lands in response to a rash of violent confrontations that had broken out between American settlers and Native American tribes.

In addition, the first president injected his office into subjects that were a matter of discretion, knowing that they were likely to establish a precedent for other chief executives going forward. The best example of this occurred in legislative affairs, an area in which Washington was clearly reluctant to intercede. For example, Washington exercised his veto power exactly once during his first term. On April 5, 1792, he vetoed a law passed by Congress that would have increased the apportionment of seats to northern states in the House of Representatives; he believed that it did so by exceeding the total number of seats proscribed by the Constitution (no more than one representative "for thirty thousand"). President Washington understood that in taking that step, some would believe he was siding with the southern interests of Randolph and Secretary of State Jefferson over Secretary of Treasury Hamilton and Secretary of War Knox. But it was more important to Washington that the first and only veto of his first term not be overridden, as that would expose the president as weak and unimportant in the legislative process. He got his wish: five days after the veto, Congress threw out the bill and settled on the more conservative interpretation of apportionment that did not give an additional House member to the eight states which had the largest fraction left over after dividing by 30,000.

Washington also exercised presidential discretion in other matters. Though Jefferson insisted that the creation of a new national bank was beyond the authority granted by the Constitution, Washington sided with Hamilton on the matter and signed the legislation creating such a bank on February 25, 1792. And while Washington was reluctant to use force to put down grain farmers who felt they were shouldering too large a percentage of the national debt, he issued his first proclamation for calling up state militias on August 7, 1791, after Pennsylvania state officials failed to take the initiative themselves.

In many ways, the pursuit of Washington's second objective—to ensure that the other branches could effectively check the presidency—would prove far more challenging given his enormous popularity. His election victory was largely a product of the faith that politicians of nearly every stripe had in him. Ardent supporters of the new Constitution were convinced his stature would help protect the new government when it faltered; opponents hoped he would be transparent about his own misgivings, and possibly even admit when the new constitutional system required rethinking on a large scale. The faith of all rested squarely on Washington to do what was right. In such a popular president's hands, the executive might become the type of dangerous authority that threatened to undermine the purposes of the revolution that made him even possible.

Right at the outset, Washington refused symbolic shows of authority. He rejected being referred to as "your highness" or "your majesty": The Constitution prohibited royal titles, and so "Mr. President" became Washington's preferred way of being addressed. In pursuit of more open government, he referred to government officials as "servants" of the people; he prohibited the appointment of government officials' relatives and friends to public posts; and he even established the tradition of senatorial courtesy by deferring to senators on judicial appointments in their home states or objections to lower-level executive appointments. Many of these actions carried symbolic importance given Washington's extreme popularity.

All this first-term political activity occurred against a backdrop of confusion about Washington's real intentions with regard to staying in office beyond the election of 1792. From the outset of his administration, Washington had expressed reluctance to serve more than one term as president. Indeed, he had originally planned to serve "as short a time as possible; less, he hoped, than a full four-year term."[64]

Several factors were at work in his reaching that conclusion. When he first took office in April 1789, Washington was 57 years old—already 15 years past the average life expectancy of males at that time. Less than two months after his first inauguration, Washington had a tumor removed from his thigh that had made it painful for the president to either walk or sit. A similar, but milder tumor appeared halfway through his first term. In the spring of 1790, he came down with influenza and pneumonia, which significantly impacted his hearing. As Washington himself wrote to David Stuart of that period:

> I have already had, within less than a year, two severe attacks, the last worse than the first. A third, more than probably, will put me to sleep with my fathers . . . Within the last twelve months I have undergone more, and severer sickness than thirty preceding years afflicted me with . . . I still feel the remains of the violent affection of my lungs; the cough, pain in my breast, and shortness of breathing not having entirely left me . . . [65]

Additionally, Washington had survived recurrent bouts of malaria and tuberculosis, and even one run-in with smallpox. And while he had survived all these life-threatening illnesses, they had taken a toll on his physical health. In April of 1790, a more difficult bout of pneumonia made him just that much more eager to relinquish the presidency.[66]

There were other factors as well. The financial condition of Mount Vernon had grown ever more precarious in the years since the war. Frequent battles between cabinet members (especially Hamilton and Jefferson) had worn him down during his first term as president as well. And yet all of these challenges paled in comparison to Washington's greatest concern: that continuing in office would pose a threat to his personal reputation as a man of honor and virtue. Washington was determined not to leave the capital sullied by accusations that his motives were anything but sincere and driven by a sense of duty to the public. And yet he was inviting exactly that criticism if he remained in power.

Washington's concept of honor had been shaped during the revolutionary era—like many other prominent Americans who came of age in the 1770s, he wanted the new country to succeed, "but not at the cost of honor or virtue."[67] What did that honor now demand of him as he neared the end of his initial term as president? External rank and reputation were motivating factors for Washington, and public recognition of his achievements was never far from his mind. At the same time, there is considerable evidence that Washington tended to hold the nation's honor above his own.[68] He studiously cultivated the perception that he placed the nation first and his own interests second. As president, he was determined not to squander that perception in order to achieve short-term political victories that might soon be overtaken by subsequent events, if not outright forgotten.

His career had never been immune from criticisms that he occasionally defined his own sense of honor in ways that conveniently ignored his own moral failings or contradictions. In the most notable example, his continued ownership of slaves at Mount Vernon (he owned more than three hundred in the 1790s) was a moral failing Washington had in common with many of his fellow residents of the Commonwealth of Virginia; even after the revolution, he refused to free them. Additionally, Washington had been a member of elitist groups like the Society of the Cincinnati, the Freemasons, and a gentlemen's club in Williamsburg, and he steadfastly refused to leave them in the face of legitimate criticisms that they celebrated the kind of royalty and aristocracy that the American revolution fought against.[69] Thomas Jefferson, John Adams and Benjamin Franklin were among the many who leveled criticisms at Washington for his membership in such organizations. Finally, while Washington championed the free press in his public statements, he often bristled at their negative coverage, especially when it became clear that members of his own administration were feeding opposition newspapers during his presidency.

These failings aside, Washington's commitment to honor and virtue provided him with a strategic advantage over contemporaries who pursued short-term political victories as a matter of right. On occasion, he worked from the inside to reform such elitist societies. Based on Washington's interventions, the Society of the Cincinnati passed reforms that would discontinue the hereditary part of its own constitutional provisions.[70] Later during the post-revolutionary period, Washington would reframe events to fit his conception of honor. While the violent farmers behind the Shays' Rebellion believed it was they who were championing the cause of honor by highlighting grievances that were ignored by their own government (they claimed "it was a matter of honor to rectify such injustices,"), Washington believed that the government's inability to stifle the rebels was the true slight to national honor. The effort to create a new constitution was consistent with that theme.

Washington's capacity to see the qualities of honor lurking in many

of these early American political conflicts allowed him to find motiva-
tion and resources to wage political battles when it seemed like the res-
ervoir had otherwise run dry. The energy he brought to these conflicts
no doubt shocked friends and foes alike. In truth, keeping others off balance stands among Washington's greatest (though perhaps least recognized) strengths. And it would play a critical role in keeping him in the
presidency long after his enemies believed possible. On this one score,
Washington surprised even himself with a capacity to endure.

The Presidential Election of 1792

As Washington's first term drew to a close, the ledger of his administration included many successes. As such, all of "Washington's visceral
instincts told him it was time to leave office."[71] For the first time ever,
the US government was on a sound financial basis thanks to Congress's
passage of the Tariff Act of 1789, and just as importantly, the Collections
Act of 1789. Together, those two laws established the US Customs Service and designated various ports of entry to help guard against illegal
smuggling. The federal government was also empowered to issue federal
bonds at its discretion. Government competence was also on display in
May of 1792, when officials brought an imploded stock market bubble
more or less under control.[72]

Longer-term projects for the new nation were moving forward as
well. The site of the new US capital (roughly fifteen miles from Mount
Vernon) had been determined in negotiations between Hamilton, Madison, and Jefferson. By March of 1792, Secretary of State Jefferson was
able to announce that ten new amendments (the "Bill of Rights") had
been ratified and enshrined in the Constitution. Western settlement was
proceeding as well, as increasing numbers of settlers continued to move
west into the territories while the Washington administration pursued
(with mixed success) a policy of assimilation through treaties with Native American tribes. "The nation's condition," Washington wrote in late
1791, "was improving and tranquility reigns." According to David Stewart, it was "likely the high point of his feelings about the presidency," [73]
if only because such conditions enhanced his prospects for a dignified
escape from the capital and a permanent return to private life.

To be sure, the Washington administration faced considerable unfinished business on several other fronts. Under the best of circumstances, most presidents find it difficult to tie up all the loose ends that exist before the end of a single presidential term.[74] For Washington, the size of the task was so great that he was unable to tackle even a small percentage of his duties. Consider that with an empty government laid out before him, Washington had been single-handedly responsible for appointing all federal officials for three executive departments (Treasury; Foreign Affairs, later renamed "State"; and War) as well as an attorney general and a postmaster general; all six members of the US Supreme Court;[75] more than twenty jurists to staff the federal district courts; and several Article IV territorial judges as well. Moreover, several officials and judges resigned from their posts mid-term, forcing the president to keep submitting new nominees to the Senate in an endless cycle of filling positions.

Foreign affairs presented a minefield as well, as Washington sought to maintain a fierce policy of neutrality. As a former general who possessed an acute understanding of military power, Washington was certain the United States remained far too weak and unstable to fight a war against any of the European superpowers. Like many Americans, he viewed the French Revolution as a mostly positive development;[76] nevertheless, Washington was determined to avoid any outward show of support that might threaten important commercial ties with Great Britain. The president even believed a formal proclamation of neutrality might be necessary, though depending on its wording and timing, such a statement might provoke an unwanted response from France or Britain. Meanwhile, Spain, which controlled lands west of the Mississippi river, had attempted to slow the influx of American settlers to the region. US military forces were already stretched thin, as federal soldiers faced armed insurrections from frontier farmers in Western Pennsylvania and elsewhere who bitterly opposed the federal tax on whiskey.

Washington certainly knew that if he agreed to serve a second term, he would be forced to undergo significant personal costs. Some of these costs would be deeply personal: most notably, the negative effect his continued presidency would have on the maintenance and finances of his Mount Vernon estate. During his first term, Washington spent considerable time trekking the 250 miles from New York City to Mount Vernon, tending to repairs on the buildings and gardening more generally. When the market for tobacco declined, the estate was suddenly forced to grow mixed crops including wheat, corn, and even cotton and silk. These were generally less labor-intensive than tobacco crops, leading to a surplus of slave labor at Mount Vernon; still, Washington refused to break up slave families, and so the estate struggled to make ends meet. Washington's frequent absences did not make things easier.

The president's own physical health remained a significant concern as well. Washington told Thomas Jefferson that he really felt himself "growing old, his bodily health less firm, his memory, already bad, becoming worse . . ."[77] It was bad enough that the president was slowly becoming deaf, and his eyesight was weakening. But the lapses in memory were especially troubling, and for Washington, his overall health situation seemed "scarcely tolerable."[78]

And then there was Martha Washington. Though she had willingly hosted many affairs of state in the nation's temporary capitals during his first term in office, she complained often both to her husband and friends about the toll so many of these events took on her daily existence. A series of rigid protocol rules forbade her and the president from accepting invitations to dine in private homes: this caused her serious loneliness when she was in New York City, the first capital of the United States. Even mundane activities like shopping or taking her grandchildren to the circus were recorded by the press. Moreover, the first lady feared that her aging husband would not survive another term.[79] Martha Washington had never been excited about her husband running for the first term, and she had no thoughts of quietly deferring to her husband if he planned to stay president for an additional four years.

These were the stakes as Washington understood them in early 1792, and they all pointed in favor of departure. That spring the president informed cabinet secretaries Jefferson, Hamilton, and Knox, as well as Attorney General Edmund Randolph and James Madison, that he planned to step down at the end of the present term.[80] In June he asked Madison to draft a "farewell address" for him to deliver to the public. The congressman from Virginia knew Washington wanted to leave, but he still felt he was responding to a genuine request from a president who had not yet made his decision either way.

And yet just as Washington was preparing to publicly declare his intentions to depart, conflicts between his secretary of the treasury and the secretary of state seemed to explode into an all-out partisan war. While Madison was dutifully drafting Washington's swan song, the president watched as Jefferson and Hamilton waged battles over the wisdom of creating a national bank, as well as the role state governments should play in governing. The rivalry moved into foreign policy as well: Hamilton denounced the French minister Edmond-Charles Genet for attacking British ships and supported the president's policy of neutrality between those two nations; Jefferson favored the French revolutionaries and the unstable government they had created there. The conflict had north-versus-south implications as well, with Jefferson and Madison representing the southern views, as opposed to the nationalistic furor of Hamilton the New Yorker.

George Washington was genuinely "astonished by the level of rancor between his two brilliant lieutenants" and worried that the republic itself might soon be at risk if it continued at its current pace.[81] Seeking advice from outside government, he turned to Eliza Powell, a close friend and confidante. Powell summoned the images of "tyrants biding their time in the shadows" in telling Washington that his resignation as president "would elate the enemies of good government."[82] Secretary of State Jefferson, while still a member of Washington's cabinet, had secretly set up a newspaper to attack all of the president's policies that had been shaped by Hamilton. To Jefferson, this was not disloyalty, "but rather a greater loyalty to the republican ideals of the revolution."[83]

Far from blaming the growing partisanship on Washington's failed leadership, Jefferson, Hamilton and Madison all pleaded with the president to stay by making the same argument: that "no one else would do" and that the union essentially rested on Washington's shoulders.[84] Thomas Jefferson wrote directly to Washington, urging him in panic-struck language to serve a second term:

> I can scarcely contemplate a more incalculable evil than the breaking of the union into two or more parts . . . the confidence of the whole

union is centered in you . . . North and South will hang together if
they have you to hang on."[85]

Echoing Jefferson's views, Madison told the president that these partisan trends made him "all the more indispensable" as he was the only one
who could mediate the emerging divisions.[86] Hamilton then summed it
up for Washington in especially dramatic terms: "The impression is uniform—that your declining would be deplored as the greatest evil that
could befall the country at this present juncture."[87]

By late August, Washington had become convinced that these battles
might very well rip the country apart without his leadership. Jefferson
and Hamilton had each made clear that the nation's "fragile equilibrium"
would be impossible to maintain otherwise.[88] George Washington still
wanted to return to Mount Vernon, but he would only do so if it did not
mean "damaging the public's faith in the office" that he had worked so
hard to establish.[89] That would not be possible.

Washington kept hesitating to make a formal announcement. As late
as November 1, his closest friends and advisors did not yet know with
certainty what Washington had decided. Meanwhile, no other candidate
had come forward, as his decision to stand for reelection seemed to be
a foregone conclusion. The transformation in Washington's thinking
had coincided with the birth of the first political party system, pitting
Hamilton's Federalists against the Democratic-Republican interests
favored by Jefferson and Madison. George Washington reluctantly set
aside Madison's first draft of a farewell address and resigned himself to
his fate.

On the outside, Washington put up a brave face. But among his close
confidants, there was no mistaking how he truly felt about once again
delaying his final retirement to Mount Vernon. In a letter to his long-
time friend and neighbor, Henry Lee, the president refused to mince his
words:

But to say I feel pleasure from the prospect of commencing another
tour of duty would be a departure from the truth; . . . it was after a
long and painful conflict in my own breast, that I was withheld . . .
from requesting in time, that no vote might be thrown away upon

me, it being my fixed determination to return to the walks of private life at the end of my term.[90]

Washington would face even more troubling decisions in the years to come.

CHAPTER 2

Decision (1793–1797)

The Second Term and the Decision to Leave Office

The second inauguration of George Washington as president of the United States took place on March 4, 1793. The centerpiece of the event was the president's formal address, which he delivered in Philadelphia's Senate Chamber Hall at approximately noon. The speech was notable for its brevity: a mere 133 words long, it remains the shortest inaugural day speech ever given by a US president.[1] To be sure, Washington's speeches had never been long: his first inaugural address contained a mere 1,419 words and clocked in at just ten minutes. Even by those standards, however, his second inaugural address was remarkably short. It was a day of mixed emotions for Washington, who had never dreamed of becoming president of the United States for one term, much less the second term he was now undertaking. Yet the nation's democratic experiment was still at risk in 1792, and the pleadings of Jefferson, Hamilton, and others had convinced him to remain in office, if only to keep the peace in an increasingly fragmented nation.

Washington's 133 words at least provided some indication of what he valued most going into his second term. Above all, he hoped the office of the presidency would remain respected, not just because it held solemn powers under the Constitution, but because it was duly accountable to the polity it served. Directing the address to his "fellow citizens," Washington spoke briefly of the road he had just traveled in his first term: that to be reelected was a "distinguished honor" in that the people had offered him the "confidence" to carry on. He then turned to the constitutional oath he was about to take,[2] and mentioned the possibility that the government might "violate willingly or knowingly" the injunctions required of him. If that happened, Washington warned, he must suffer both "constitutional punishment" as well as the "upbraidings" of all who were present that day. On that somber note, Washington took the oath of office and returned to the president's living space and office at the Robert Morris house on High Street, barely a third of a mile from where the ceremony took place.

One could not have drawn a starker contrast than that between the Washington who was sworn in that day in March of 1793 and the man who had left the Continental Army and returned to private life nearly a decade earlier. When Washington resigned his position as the Continental Army's military commander on December 23, 1783, the fifty-one-year-old Virginian had declared he was "happy in the confirmation of our Independence and Sovereignty, and pleased with the opportunity afforded the United States of becoming a respectable Nation." He called the act of surrendering his military command "the last solemn act of my Official life," and by all accounts he meant it. When he departed for Mount Vernon that same day, he had no reason to think he eventually would be pressed into politics, much less drafted to serve two full terms as the nation's president. And yet the problems of the United States that demanded so much of his attention during his first term would soon give way to even more significant problems in his second term.

A Second Term for a Reluctant Public Servant

As the newly reelected president, Washington faced partisan divisions as well as threats from within and abroad. Every month that passed under the new Constitution helped to convince more Americans and foreigners alike that the United States would endure. To maintain that level of reassuring stability remained a challenge, however. Though Washington had reluctantly endorsed establishment of the First National Bank of the United States during his first term of office, hard economic decisions remained. As secretary of the treasury, Hamilton was convinced that manufacturing faced a "promising future" in the United States,[3] but policies that promoted that industry would favor the wealthy in the short term and thus prove unpopular with a large segment of the population. On the foreign policy front, the president's desire to maintain US neutrality among the European powers would be severely tested as well.

In forging ahead with his second-term agenda, President Washington would soon be hampered by a much weaker cabinet of officers available to supply him with advice. Secretary of State Jefferson resigned from the cabinet as 1793 neared its end. He was replaced by Edmund Randolph, who was himself forced out by a scandal in August of 1795.[4] Secretary of War Henry Knox and Treasury Secretary Alexander Hamilton also made plans to depart the cabinet in the middle of Washington's second term. By any measure, Washington's second-term Cabinet was "markedly inferior to his original one," especially after Jefferson's departure.[5] Six straight candidates turned down the chance to run the State Department after Randolph; eventually Secretary of War Timothy Pickering—in his current position for less than a year—agreed to switch over and take the vacant position.

Without a strong cabinet, President Washington would be less prepared to deal with the two greatest challenges of his second term: (1) violent protests over the whiskey tax in the West; and (2) the growing controversy surrounding negotiation and passage of the Jay Treaty. The events that led to the so-called "Whiskey Rebellion" dated back to Washington's first term, when the federal government's imposition of a whiskey tax to help pay down war debts had led to violent protests by aggrieved farmers against tax collectors. The insurrection reached a climax in July 1794, compelling Washington to personally lead an army to suppress the insurgency with the help of thirteen thousand state militiamen.[6] All these events occurred against the backdrop of heightened partisanship back in the capital. Even though the Democratic-Republican societies created in 1793 and 1794 to promote Jeffersonian Republicanism were not actually responsible for the farmers' insurgency, Washington remained convinced that they had played a significant role as agitators.[7]

The Jay Treaty with Great Britain had also exacerbated the partisan wars. Submitted to the US Senate for ratification in June of 1795, the agreement negotiated by Chief Justice (and special envoy) John Jay had failed to resolve American grievances about shipping rights and the British impressment of American soldiers at sea.[8] It did, however, fulfill many other US objectives, including the withdrawal of British troops from the Northwest territory, the arbitration of continued wartime disputes, and the granting of "most favored nation" status to the United States. That final concession provided Americans with expanded trading rights in British colonies in the Caribbean.

Still, the treaty's failure to address the impressment of Americans (or to compensate southern planters for slaves who had escaped to British lines) gave Jefferson and his supporters all the ammunition they needed to proclaim the treaty a virtual surrender to Great Britain. French government officials thought the agreement violated treaties between the two nations, and so they too were outraged. Once the Jay Treaty was ratified by a narrow two-thirds majority (20–10) in the Senate, it became a central issue in the partisan wars pitting Federalists against Jeffersonians. President Washington rejoiced in the treaty's passage because it helped enforce American sovereignty over the Northwest territory by diplomatic means, avoiding the war with Great Britain that he feared more than anything. Still, even after its ratification, he continued to take the opposition seriously, not because he gave actual weight to their objections, but because they might actually persuade the French government that the treaty was somehow calculated to favor Great Britain.[9] No one understood better than Washington how false perceptions could undermine his continued efforts to maintain neutrality in disputes among the European superpowers.

He was also pleased at ongoing developments in US relations with Spain. Frustrated at that nation's continued willingness to stand in the way of American expansion into the Southwest, the Washington administration endorsed the Pinckney Treaty (finalized in October of 1795), which guaranteed unrestricted American navigation of the Mississippi River with the right of deposit at New Orleans. Jeffersonians complained that this treaty, too, had come at the expense of more positive Franco-American relations.[10]

Still, by late 1795, all these developments had taken a toll on Washington's image as a leader who had long managed to stand above the fray of partisan politics. Jeffersonians now viewed the president as a "party leader"[11] who was "a Federalist in fact if not in name."[12] After opponents in Congress tried and failed in their attempts to withhold funds necessary to put the Jay Treaty into effect, President Washington only added fuel to the fire when he declared that "he was no longer interested in inviting another Democratic-Republican into his Cabinet."[13] To be sure, Jefferson and Madison could not see what historians like Garry Wills later did: that "the pressure of events was carrying America along with [revolutionary] France, and Washington had to lean in the opposite direction to arrive at neutrality."[14]

George Washington's relationship with the press soured considerably during this period. Slowly, he came to regard the opposition press as "an evasive and disuniting force" that provided "only one side" of the story."[15] Unlike in his first term, Washington now had little patience for the harsh criticisms that would inevitably come with a free press.[16] Week after week, he watched his name vilified in the Republican press, and his critics were especially harsh after he signed the Jay Treaty, calling him "a dupe of Hamilton" and "senile."[17] One Republican-leaning newspaper suggested that the Jay Treaty proved Washington has in fact "supported the redcoats all along."[18] Meanwhile the *Philadelphia Aurora*, an anti-Federalist newspaper started in 1794, accused Washington of ignoring the masses by "seeking the greatest for the least number possessing the greatest wealth."[19]

The president was clearly upset that a former member of his own cabinet (Jefferson) and a once trusted advisor (Madison) had created a new newspaper (*The National Gazette*) with the express purpose of attacking his policies.[20] George Washington had once trusted Madison to assist him on the most sensitive of matters, including the crafting of a farewell address in 1792. Still, as early as 1794, "things had deteriorated so totally between the President and the erudite little Congressman" that the mere mention of Madison's name drove Washington into fits.[21] To the president, all debate was fair as decision-making progressed, but once policy was actually set, he felt "all citizens were obliged to give their support."[22] And yet for most of his second term he still did not counterattack in public,[23] aware that his legacy as a proponent of the free press was at stake. Washington's physical stamina was also tested during his second term, and it had not fared favorably. In January of 1795, he wrote to his longtime friend Edmund Pendleton that he had little energy left to mount a sustained response to such criticisms:

... although I have no cause to complain of the want of health, I can religiously aver, that no man was ever more tired of public life, or more devoutly wished for retirement than I do.[24]

No one privy to such correspondence could have doubted Washington's heartfelt longing for the final chapter of his career in public service to conclude sooner rather than later.

Washington's silence in the face of such partisan attacks only further exasperated his growing number of critics. Indeed, Jeffersonian-backed newspapers grew increasingly frustrated that Washington remained the most popular figure in the United States. Accordingly, the attacks grew even more personal. From Republican newspapers in the South came stories of George Washington "betraying the revolution and craving a crown."[25] And there were increasingly bitter criticisms in the press about the Washingtons' lifestyle.[26] Perhaps the most painful comments of all came from Thomas Paine, who on July 30, 1796, published a bitter letter bashing Washington on every front: he denounced him as an incompetent general and hypocrite who had encouraged adulation and vanity.[27] Many Americans bristled at the attack on a living legend, and there was scant evidence that Paine's words did any damage to Washington's political standing. There was, however, considerable damage to Washington's psyche. Paine and Washington had always had a strained relationship; but after August of 1796, their relationship had effectively ended.

Nor did Washington's relationship with Jefferson fare well amid such pronounced and sustained attacks. In a private letter sent to his former cabinet member in Monticello in July of 1796, Washington made clear to Jefferson just how frustrated he was that the partisan attacks had grown so personal:

I had no conception that parties would or even could go to the length I have been witness to; nor did I believe until lately, that it was within the bounds of probability, hardly within those of possibility that ... I should be accused of being the enemy of one nation, and subject to the influence of another; and to prove it, that every act of my administration would be tortured, and the grossest and most insidious misrepresentations of them be made, by giving one side only of a subject . . . But enough of this. I have already gone further in the expression of my feelings than I intended.[28]

Indeed, Washington went no further. He would never speak to Jefferson again.

Washington's Farewell Address

When President Washington asked James Madison to draft a farewell address in 1792, he was genuinely undecided as to whether he would stand for reelection that fall. Four years later, Washington had no intention of seeking Madison's help on this or any other matter.

In 1796, his departure seemed far more likely, if not a foregone conclusion. With Madison now an adversary, the president turned instead to Hamilton. Washington's instructions to his former aide seemed straightforward: he wanted the address to state in plain terms what challenges the nation now faced, and to spell out the dangers to self-government of vesting continued power in a popular leader.[29] Washington provided Hamilton with Madison's rough draft, though he also included with it his own edits and additions, "many of which Hamilton, of all people, [would later] cut for sounding too bitter."[30]

The former secretary of the treasury responded with two drafts for Washington's review. The first tinkered with, but essentially retained, most of Madison's original draft in hopes of limiting Republican criticisms that were likely to follow. But Hamilton also provided Washington with an entirely new draft that he had written on his own. This second draft incorporated a small amount of the language from Madison's original version, but then went on to ruminate about the greater threats to the American experiment posed by excessive political "party spirit" and "geographical distinctions." Washington and Hamilton were both thinking about the Democratic-Republicans in this part of the address; indeed, it could be read as a virtual "demolition of Thomas Jefferson and his political party."[31]

Per Washington's instructions, this second draft warned that the combination of popularity and power in one executive posed perhaps the greatest threat to liberty.[32] Washington did not want to be considered an exception to this rule; rather, he was a living example of why rotation in office was so necessary. The second draft also dedicated far more attention to the question of foreign affairs, as it warned against long-term alliances with other nations.[33] Hamilton believed these "reflections and sentiments" would "wear well."[34]

Though Hamilton was the critical engine behind this second draft, the ideas he articulated were Washington's from beginning to end.[35] As the historian Joseph Ellis would later write, "It was a collaborative effort in which Hamilton was the draftsman who wrote most of the words, while Washington was the author whose ideas prevailed throughout."[36] For example, Hamilton chose not to emphasize all of Washington's accomplishments as president—the addition of a Bill of Rights and five new states, the securing of the western frontier, and staying out of war[37]—as he knew the president had little interest in turning the moment into a celebratory lap and would likely delete that material anyway. It turns out Hamilton understood his old boss's thinking quite well. The president indicated that he preferred Hamilton's second draft, though he did ask him to add a section on the importance of education.[38]

In early September, Washington told friends and associates that there would be no consideration of a third term in office. He then revealed his decision to the public by publishing his farewell address in the form of a letter dated September 19, 1796.[39] In making this historic announcement, Washington was aware that he was leaving Vice President Adams, Thomas Jefferson, Patrick Henry, and a handful of others to wage a battle over who would succeed him. Though Adams's position made him the heir apparent in many people's eyes, few thought Washington would try to influence his selection.[40]

The final version of Washington's published address offered only a limited explanation of the factors that had gone into the decision itself. In Washington's own words, he had carefully weighed the benefits of retirement to himself personally ("the shade of retirement is as necessary to me as it will be welcome") versus the costs of his continued service in an increasingly partisan and divided capital. Based on that calculus, he believed his continued service as president was no longer

necessary; that "patriotism does not forbid" retirement; and that unlike
four years earlier, the public would not disapprove of the decision. He
then dedicated the bulk of his address to the great questions facing the
United States. Taken as a whole, this thirty-two-page handwritten address remains the most important—and perhaps the most memorable—
of George Washington's public speeches.

Notwithstanding the words Washington actually offered for public consumption, what were the real factors that led to Washington's
self-imposed retirement? The former general did not realistically fear
the possibility of electoral defeat, as he would have won a third term
handily, though perhaps not unanimously.[41] No longer an unqualified
supporter of the current president, even Thomas Jefferson recognized
that Washington's power and influence over the people continues to
"outweigh them all."[42]

Rather, there were multiple factors that figured into the decision:

Washington's health. George Washington would be approaching sev-
enty years old near the end of a theoretical third term. Dating back to his
first term, observers had already noticed an "uncharacteristic listlessness" about Washington as well as a more gradual decline in his endur-
ance.[43] Washington was equally concerned about his mental stamina: he
told Jay that the years "had worn away [his] mind" more than his body.[44]
From Washington's perspective, he no longer possessed the physical or
mental stamina needed to weather and/or parry attacks from Paine and
others who were willing to savage him in the press without fear of con-
sequence.[45] Given Washington's desire to leave office on his own terms,
he was understandably wary of continuing any further.[46]

Increased partisanship. As noted above, the increasingly contentious
political climate in the capital made his second term a daily trial, and
even more contentiousness was expected over the next four years. A
Washington administration would clearly have less capacity to weather
those challenges during a third term. Certainly, the government itself
would be weaker, as the number of well-respected figures willing to serve
the federal government had dwindled considerably by 1796. Freed of the
loyalty requirements imposed on cabinet members, Jefferson had helped

raise public opinion against the Washington administration during its second term and he would continue to do so. And despite Washington's unwavering support, passage of the Jay Treaty had inflamed the growth of two opposing parties in every single state in the union.

Maintaining an accountable executive. The same concerns that drove Washington to abandon the Articles of Confederation—the lack of an effective executive—were at the forefront of Washington's mind when he finally elected to retire. The Constitution had restored power to the executive, but at what cost to democracy? For the better part of eight years, President Washington had worked to "bridge the shift from kingship to an executive authority derived from the people."[47] Many of his words and actions were calculated to counter fears that his administration would take on the trappings of monarchy. But he could not countenance any weakening of the executive, lest the constitutional experiment be allowed to fail. This was not an easy balance for any president to strike; it was especially hard for Washington, who was treated like a near deity: Twice elected unanimously, Washington enjoyed the overwhelming adulation of the public. Fears of an "idolatrous and exclusive attachment" to the man were running rampant.[48] If such a powerful authority as Washington remained in power too long, comparisons to an unfettered monarchy would only increase.

Washington's personal legacy. Notwithstanding Washington's image as a man characterized by self-denial and humility, he had a substantial ego when it came to his reputation and the way he would be remembered. Washington was obsessed with his legacy, and he never lost sight of how posterity would judge his reputation for personal honor and integrity after he passed from the political scene.[49] To be sure, "people did not admire the conquering Caesar in him."[50] Rather, they admired him because he had exercised the authority vested in him in a restrained and checked way—by resigning from the army, surrendering his commission, and retiring from public life prior to his reluctant return to become the first US president.

In voluntarily relinquishing power still available to him, Washington hoped to invoke the spirit of Cincinnatus once again. The president genuinely believed that departing in 1797 would help cement his greatness in the minds of Americans. Even as late as the fall of 1796, that legacy was still secure.[51] National institutions had been well established, the Ohio country was open for settlement, and the US was at peace. Even more significant, the presidency had been established as a powerful and significant office in the brand-new constitutional system. If he were later forced out during or after an unsuccessful third term, it would give credence to his enemies and their partisan attacks. A continued escalation of attacks from Paine and others might even leave a stain on his reputation that would sway the public's thinking. Such a scenario was not impossible to imagine; by leaving on his own terms the following year, he would both embody the principle of limited government, and at the same time, he would be remembered for putting the needs of the nation above his own personal glory.

Preserving the principle of rotation in the nation's highest office. From the moment when he first assumed the presidency in 1789, George Washington was committed to the principle of rotation in office in accordance with the "republican spirit of the Constitution" in which power was retained by the people.[52] He wanted his departure to demonstrate that republican succession could be achieved peaceably through free and fair elections. By modeling that very process, he would help the country "rise above the squabbles of the moment" as well as highlight ideals and traditions that were anti-monarchial in nature.[53] A third term would pose a serious threat to those ideals by inviting the possibility of two regrettable scenarios: (1) he might die in office, following the path of most other monarchs before him; or (2) he might be forced from office due to scandal, incapacity or some other factor. Either way of exiting would provide a blow against executive authority at a time when the republic was still new and fragile.

A Precedent is Born

George Washington never deviated from his true intent to use his departure as a "didactic opportunity" for the citizenry. By modeling the free and peaceful transfer of power to a new president, he hoped to send a strong message of support for voluntary rotation in office as a "novelty in a world in which heads of states were replaced only by natural death, assassination, foreign invasion, or domestic usurpation."[54] The farewell announcement was more a valedictory address than anything else—it, too, was part of that strategic effort to frame the departure in these lofty terms. Washington was certain that his exit would likely be studied by his successors going forward, and he hoped it would "strengthen citizens' confidence in the willingness of future presidents to give up power" as well.[55]

What was the exact precedent that George Washington intended to establish by leaving when he did? Even if he had articulated his intentions with requisite specificity, the pathway to establishing a clear and unambiguous precedent for future executives to follow would prove an inexact science at best. Future executives governing under markedly different circumstances than Washington would be able to distinguish the first president's situation from their own, and thus escape any unwelcome precedent in the process. Moreover, all that assumed the president in question felt compelled to pay proper homage to Washington in the first place; it was just as possible that once a popular president was ensconced in office, he might seek to circumvent or ignore the precedent in question without exerting any effort to hide that fact.

Did Washington—who pondered leaving office on multiple occasions before actually doing so—even have a specific precedent in mind? At a minimum, he was adamant that the ending—whenever it occurred—be clear and unambiguous. If a president pondering his own departure first sought advice from Congress or raised the question first among the citizenry, he would be inviting the kind of mass adulation and support that blurred the line between a responsible chief executive and a cult hero who was demanding loyalty from the masses under the false pretext of seeking advice. Washington thus accurately foresaw the problem President Lyndon Baines Johnson fostered in 1968, when he was considering retirement while simultaneously campaigning for votes in Democratic state primaries. What vote percentage would be sufficient to keep him running for reelection? Washington believed it was important to "leave no room" for debate over whether he really planned to resign. Thus, after making his final decision during the summer of 1796, he presented the nation with a fait accompli.[56] He believed a free and voluntary exit by any future president should be based on the best interests of the nation, and not on the outcome of a last-minute plebiscite.

Another concern was how to define the ideal length of presidential service. In a free republic marked by constitutional restraints and accountability, how much service threatened the transformation of popular presidents into the functional equivalent of monarchs removable only by death or incapacity? To Washington, there was nothing especially meaningful about a president serving two four-year terms before retiring. (Indeed, Washington actually served less than eight years, as his first term began on April 30, 1789, and concluded on March 4, 1793). Rejecting Hamilton's position from the constitutional convention that presidents should serve for life, Washington focused more on a scenario that might unduly undermine executive authority: a president who has committed no impeachable offense being pressured to resign against his will for political or partisan reasons. Far more important than the exact length of service was the nature of the decision: *Washington believed above all that the act of stepping down should be voluntary.* It was this critical factor of "voluntariness" that he hoped to preserve. And so, as Joseph Ellis argues, Washington left office

> under his own power, not dying in office like a monarch, making the simple point in dramatic fashion that republican leaders, no matter how indispensable, were all disposable . . . [57]

In 1796, the very idea of the United States without Washington was unimaginable to the public. But Washington saw the need for a formidable central government headed by a strong chief executive, and he did not want to see presidents chased from office by impeachment or scandal. Chief executives who held onto their office for as long as possible might never leave except by death or incapacity; from Washington's perspective, this posed the greatest danger of all to the American experiment.

If scandal or vehement partisan opposition could prematurely drive a president from office, extreme challenges to the nation such as the looming threat of war or a major economic crisis might well have the opposite effect, keeping a president in office longer than he would have otherwise preferred. Washington weighed that possibility as well before he made his decision to retire. That summer, the United States faced enormous challenges, all of which the president could have cited as justification for remaining in office. Didn't the government require steady and experienced leadership to take on such immense challenges? The fact that he left when he did helped to safeguard the principle that no future president could ever be considered indispensable. And it promoted the democratic practice of rotating chief executives when circumstances might have dictated otherwise.

George Washington exited the nation's capital in March of 1797, handing off the presidency to his vice president, John Adams. By following the example of Cincinnatus, he enhanced his legacy. He might have even gained some power in the process, as have other reluctant heroes who denied the path of despotism. It is a dynamic with a long history indeed. What was the impact of Washington's decision on his successors?

CHAPTER 3

Aftermath (1797–1951)

The Presidents Who Followed Washington and the Precedent They Followed

George Washington hoped his successors would take some lessons from his departure. But he also knew that the unique circumstances of his presidency—a military hero responsible for victory in the Revolutionary War, the first to hold the office, twice elected without opposition—would never be repeated. Contemporaries who opposed the president on numerous policy matters reconciled themselves to the reality that the presidency belonged to Washington for as long as he wanted it. Not even Franklin Delano Roosevelt at the height of his popularity in the mid-1930s could have accurately made such a claim.

As was discussed in Chapter 1, most delegates at the constitutional convention initially favored limiting the president's service to a single term (length still to be determined) as a means of protecting the young republic against the threat of a corrupt executive. James Madison and several other delegates had opposed provisions that afforded the president continued eligibility for office. How then did reeligibility emerge in the final draft of the document? Here again, Washington's quiet work behind the scenes proved decisive. The former general believed that the possibility of reelection—combined with the threat of impeachment and removal by Congress—would serve as an effective check against unbridled executive wrongdoing. As every delegate believed Washington was slated to become the nation's first president, he held outsized influence to shape those terms accordingly.

Nearly a decade later, Washington departed the presidency hopeful that future chief executives would view their continued eligibility to run for reelection under the Constitution as an effective check on their powers, and not simply as a blanket invitation to remain in office indefinitely. In his Farewell Address, Washington refused to specify the proper length of time that an executive should serve in office. Instead, he focused on his own specific circumstances and the needs of the country at that precise moment in its history. Of course, by emphasizing the need for discretion and judgment, his own actions would allow for multiple interpretations by future presidents.

If Washington intended to create an instructive example for his successors, why did he leave so many fundamental questions unanswered:

- Did he intend his departure to offer a proscription against presidents serving three consecutive terms or against a third term, whenever it might occur?
- Did he hope that once a president left office, he would never return to the federal government in any other capacity? Was he opposed to retired chief executives taking on additional roles in any of the three branches of government?
- Did Washington's model for departure take into account the circumstances a nation faced at that particular time? Should a president serving during a declared condition of war feel emboldened to stay in the position longer when he believes it is in the interests of the nation?

Some of the precedents George Washington established in other matters exerted influence over his successors from the outset and continue to guide presidential actions today: his reliance on a cabinet of federal officials for advice and his assertion of executive privilege to protect confidential communications are prime examples. President Washington's decision to keep Vice President John Adams at arm's length proved instructive as well, as vice presidents continued to serve in mostly ceremonial roles up through the late twentieth century. Other precedents offered less strict guidelines that future presidents frequently (though by no means always) heeded. For example, some presidents have been more active than others at proposing legislation to the Congress, and some (though not all) presidents have looked within the Supreme Court

for the next chief justice. Finally, some of Washington's so-called precedents seemed to have had no influence whatsoever. For example, no future president ever led an army on the field of battle the way Washington
did as president in dealing with the Whiskey Rebellion.

Near the end of his life, Washington had the opportunity to shape
the future once more when his former military secretary, Governor Jonathan Trumbull Jr. of Connecticut, met with him in June of 1799 and
urged him to run for president once again the following year. Restless in
retirement, Washington had reluctantly accepted a commission as chief
officer in the US army in 1798 to support the Adams Administration
in preparing for a potential war against France (Washington assumed
that his own role would be mostly symbolic and that Alexander Hamilton, as senior major general, would be the de facto head of the army).
Would George Washington now reconsider his retirement and try for
a third term in office? Washington's reply to Trumbull was forthright:
"[A] man who had written a farewell address and rejected another term
in 1796 could not reverse himself without permanent damage to his reputation."[1] Once again, Washington's concern for his legacy above all else
carried the day. His failing health was clearly a factor as well—George
Washington's death on December 14, 1799, ensured he would not live
long enough to see the next election.

Not many future presidents would have been able to resist similar
calls to duty, especially when the prospects for electoral success remained so high. But unlike Washington, they would have to address the
precedent that Washington himself was still in the process of creating.

The Jeffersonian Two-Termers

Would future presidents follow Washington's example in seeking reelection at least once? The answer to that question came quickly: every one
of the next seven presidents openly sought reelection to a second term as
president, with only Adams in 1800 and Martin Van Buren in 1840 failing in their reelection bids. Still, two terms in office would not become
the overwhelming norm in presidential politics until the mid-twentieth
century: of the eighteen presidents elected during the nineteenth cen-

tury, fully half were either defeated in their reelection efforts, or refused to seek a second term in the first place.

A question surrounding Washington's precedent remained: if a president was popular enough to secure reelection to a second term, would the first president's example stand as an obstacle to his seeking a third term? Some factor must have deterred the three Virginians who succeeded John Adams (Jefferson, Madison, and Monroe) from putting their hats in the race for a third time. Each of them successfully secured reelection to a second term, helped in part by the contemporaneous decline (and dissolution) of the Federalist Party as a significant source of opposition.[2] And yet all three men departed the White House after exactly eight years in office.

Of those three cases, Jefferson's decision to retire after two terms in office has garnered by far the most attention. Two decades earlier, Jefferson had expressed distaste for the provisions of the new constitution allowing a president to run even one time for reelection. He feared that the power of removing the president "will not be exercised," thus fundamentally undermining the principle of rotation in office.[3] Visions of an American monarchy worried Jefferson throughout his career in public life, up to and including his second term in the White House.[4] Though he later evolved somewhat from that hard position, he remained convinced that the greatest danger to the republic came with the continued reelection of a president, as such a practice risked becoming "habitual," with "election for life" the most likely result.[5]

Thomas Jefferson was well aware of Washington's misgivings about extended service as president. In that vein, Jefferson interpreted Washington's departure in 1796 as tantamount to his acting on the view that presidents should not stay long and under no conditions should they stay beyond a maximum of two terms in office. As late as 1805, he told friends that "General Washington set the example of voluntary retirement after eight years . . . I shall follow it."[6] The one exception Jefferson appeared to allow was in the exceptional circumstance where "division about a successor" might somehow bring in a monarchist.[7] In his book *Presidential Term Limits in American History* (2011), Michael Korzi argues that since such a circumstance was unlikely and extreme, Jefferson's position amounted to support of the two-term precedent in nearly all respects.

In Jefferson's case, the two-term maximum proved convenient for him personally given his circumstances. While a third term was available to Washington for the asking, Jefferson's prospects for winning a third term of his own were far less certain, as "the road ahead was full of bumps and potholes."[8] The strikes against Jefferson in his second term had begun to add up. His administration continued to be blamed for the excesses of Aaron Burr's treason trial (the former vice president was acquitted). Impressment of American sailors by the British continued to stoke public outrage. Jefferson's undeclared war on Muslim pirates remained unsettled, forcing the government to consider paying a hefty ransom for American prisoners. And the controversial Embargo Act of 1807 directed at both France and Great Britain provoked bitter protests and triggered economic chaos.[9] According to Christopher Hitchens, Jefferson's second term "had seen little of the dash and initiative and glory that had marked the first one."[10]

Nor did President Jefferson enjoy the good health and stamina that was needed to stay in the job at the age of sixty-five and beyond. According to Pulitzer-winning biographer Dumas Malone, Jefferson had suffered from periodic debilitating headaches throughout his presidency; for a week during March of 1808, he was reduced to a "state of almost total incapacity" to conduct business, and his feebleness had become habitual.[11] Jefferson himself described his own state as a "listlessness of labor." In fact, Jefferson was a year older than Washington had been at the corresponding point in his administration; like Washington, he did not want to be hamstrung by worsening medical conditions in a third term.

Professor Korzi gives significant credit to Jefferson for creating the two-term precedent as a "virtual post-script" to the Constitution. In debates over the Twenty-second Amendment waged a century and a half later, several Congressmen tended to support that view as well.[12] Such a premise ignores two critical ways in which Jefferson's commitment to rotation after eight years may have been *less* principled and resolute than it might have appeared. First, unlike Washington, Jefferson's rejection of a third term was based primarily on political grounds.[13] No one can say with certainty that Jefferson would have been denied a third term, but given that his political survival was at least seriously in question,

crediting him instead of Washington for establishing a two-term precedent would be an overly generous reading of Jefferson's motives and
influence.

Second, there was the reality that Jefferson's all-but-certain successor was likely to be his closest political ally. James Madison represented
the other half of what might be termed the most important political col-
laboration between two friends in American history. Indeed, the two
statesmen from Virginia had worked together amiably for most of their
lives. Madison was not just Jefferson's loyal secretary of state for eight
years; he had corresponded with Jefferson frequently while influencing
the shape of the Constitution, and he had stood by Jefferson through the
heating up of partisan wars. President Jefferson "unquestionably" preferred Madison to anybody else as his successor.[14] Yet given that Madison had played a key role in convincing Congress to pass the ineffective
Embargo Act of 1807, President Jefferson feared that Madison's election
would be affected by it.[15] Accordingly, Jefferson took two steps that he
hoped would help Madison win their party's nomination over Monroe:
First, he announced that he would not run for a third term fully eleven
months before the election. That allowed Madison to more easily secure
the support of their mutual allies. Second, he urged Madison to turn
the necessity of ending the embargo into an electoral virtue that would
thereby work in his favor.[16] In the end, Madison won such a substantial
victory (122 electoral votes to Pinckney's 47) that it would be hard not to
view it as a vote of confidence in Jefferson's presidency.

By contrast, the beginning of John Adams's presidency could never
be confused with a third term for Washington. Though the first president occasionally dined with Adams, Washington kept his vice president at arm's length on most substantive issues, excluding him even
from routine cabinet meetings when he sought the advice of his secretaries. Washington biographer Ron Chernow suggests the reasons for
this separation were both structural and personal.[17] On the structural
side, the president took seriously the vice president's position as president of the Senate and rejected the modern notion that he was simply
the president's agent in the legislature. To keep the Senate from intrud-
ing on the presidency, Adams was kept apart from executive branch decision-making. Additionally, President Washington recalled Adams as a

congressman during the 1770s, occasionally offering vocal opposition to his military performance. For a man who demanded loyalty, this was a personal slight that he would not soon forgive. Thus, while Washington and Adams were both technically Federalists, there was little reason to think Washington's policies would simply continue under his successor.

All this meant that Jefferson's commitment to a two-term precedent offered him a painless means of propelling his vision for America forward past 1809 without facing significant political resistance and personal hardships along the way. First Madison and later Monroe left the presidency under more favorable conditions. In the case of Madison, a somewhat rocky tenure marked largely by war with Great Britain had given way to an administration that—at least according to John Adams—"acquired more glory, and established more union, than all his three predecessors."[18] Quitting while he was ahead after eight years proved an easy choice for Madison, who would not have wished to outshine his mentor Jefferson in any event.

President Monroe was a clear threat to run again in 1824. Aware of that possibility, Congress injected itself into the debate with its own stern warning: the Senate passed a resolution in early 1824 by the bipartisan vote of 36–3, limiting the president to two terms each.[19] Of dubious constitutionality, the bill never gained any support in the House. In fact, Monroe had little desire to press the two-term precedent. The fifth president thus let it be known that he would "follow the example of his predecessors" and decline reelection to a third term.[20]

Like Jefferson and Madison, Andrew Jackson was on record earlier in his political career as favoring the one-term presidency in principle. This position squared with his other frequently stated preference for a popularly elected president: both reforms fulfilled his vision for an independent but accountable chief executive. And while Jackson continued to advocate a single term for the president even after he was first elected, he saw nothing inconsistent or contradictory about running for reelection so long as the Constitution allowed him to do so.[21] Yet even for Jackson, a third term seemed like a bridge too far; like Jefferson he saw the benefits of letting his chosen successor (Vice President Martin Van Buren) carry on Jackson's policies on his behalf. At least on this one issue, Andrew Jackson chose not to buck unwritten norms. It would take a different general and the first two genuinely progressive chief executives to test Washington's precedent as it had never been tested before.

Grant, TR, and Wilson: A Precedent Wobbles, but Holds Firm

Between President Jackson's departure from the White House in early 1837 and the start of the Civil War, no president was reelected to a second term, and so the question of whether a president might serve a third term in office was effectively rendered moot during that period. In 1864, Abraham Lincoln became the first president to be reelected twice since Jackson, but his assassination cut short his presidency long before he would have been forced to consider that question. In fact, it was the Republican chief executive Ulysses S. Grant, the former union general from Missouri, who became the first president since Jackson to serve two full terms in office. Grant's fortitude and determination had made him indispensable to the union during the Civil War; might that same fortitude now be directed at taking on the seemingly indestructible two-term precedent?

Grant was far from a shoo-in to become his party's nominee for a third time in 1876: his presidency had been marked by modest successes in the first term, followed by frustrating failures in the second. Early in his administration, President Grant deployed White House resources to protect freed Black slaves and to promote the assimilation of Native Americans into American life. Yet during his second term, the north began to retreat from Reconstruction and his Native American policy fell apart, undermined by administration infighting and failed peace conferences. On the economic front, he had successfully advocated a return to the gold standard, which in turn helped to curb inflation, stabilize the dollar, and end the Panic of 1873. Those achievements left a trail of problems, however; many railroads went bankrupt, and the country experienced the onset of an industrial depression.

President Grant's second term was also replete with scandals, as corruption in the federal government appeared to run rampant. Nearly all of Grant's executive department was investigated by Congress, and few officials escaped unscathed. Grant himself was able to maintain mostly clean hands, but his gullibility, a willingness to excessively trust people, and then his failure to aggressively take on the malfeasance guaranteed that Grant would suffer politically.

Though Republicans controlled the 44th Congress by large margins, Congressional leaders were concerned that a third straight nomination for Grant might spell defeat for the party in November. Given the opportunity to deal a death blow to any nascent third-term efforts, the House of Representatives took action in December 1875. Passed by a 234–18 vote, the "Springer resolution" (named after Representative William Springer (D-IL) stated that:

> The precedent established by Washington and other Presidents of the United States in retiring from the Presidential Office after their second term has become, by universal concurrence, a part of our republican system of government . . . any departure from this time-honored custom would be unwise, unpatriotic and fraught with peril to our free institutions.[22]

Every single House Democrat and 70 of the 88 Republican House members present voted for the measure.

Aware of the negative political environment in which he found himself, Grant declined to stand for a third consecutive term in 1876. In his annual address to Congress on December 5, 1876, the president argued that his failures were "errors of judgment, not of intent." He thus informed Congress that it was *"not probable* that public affairs will ever again receive attention from me further than as a citizen of the Republic."[23]

This was hardly the definitive exit Congressional leaders had been hoping for. And when the former president and his wife returned from a two-and-a-half-year world tour to cheering crowds in late 1879, support for another Grant presidency began to gather momentum. Ulysses Grant was still just 57 years old that fall and in remarkably good health. Amazingly, the former president watched as the political stars began aligning in his favor during the first half of 1880. President Hayes had already committed to not run for reelection. Within the Republican party itself, a civil war broke out over the federal government's patronage system. On one side, forces loyal to New York Senator Roscoe Conkling (the "Stalwarts") ardently defended the current system, while the so-called "Half-breeds" led by Maine Senator James G. Blaine supported extensive civil service reform. As an ally of Conkling, Grant could count on the Stalwarts to support his candidacy, as he offered them their best shot at keeping the opposition at bay.

Grant also benefitted from a more general fear that Democratic prospects were on the rise, threatening Republican party control of the White House for the first time in a generation. Four years earlier, Rutherford Hayes and the Republicans had snatched victory from the jaws of a defeat, negotiating victory in the Electoral College even as Democratic nominee Samuel Tilden outpolled Hayes in the popular count by more than two-and-a-half million votes. Going into the next election, the national electorate appeared narrowly divided; in such a challenging climate, Grant's return to politics seemed especially fortuitous to the Republicans. For his part, Conkling took the lead in organizing Republican delegates to support Grant prior to the party's convention that June in Chicago. He was joined in this effort by the former war hero (and now Illinois Senator) John A. Logan, whose own popularity would earn him a vice presidential nod four years later.

Grant made no public comments about these efforts, though he actively encouraged them behind the scenes; at one point, he came to believe his nomination was a near certainty.[24] When Conkling formally put Grant's name into nomination on the second day of the convention, he reminded the delegates of why they had lined up for Grant in the past: "When asked which state he hails from, our sole reply shall be, he comes from Appomattox and its famous apple tree." This set off a raucous ten-minute celebration of Grant among the delegates.[25] Conkling even told friends that "nothing but an act of God could prevent Grant's nomination."[26]

Then, just as quickly as Grant's star seemed to rise, it came crashing down to earth. The reality of George Washington's unwritten two-term precedent emerged as a factor that summer, though how much of a factor remains uncertain. In a post-Civil War America where divisions between north and south persisted during and after Reconstruction, Washington remained that rare figure who continued to be celebrated in the North and South alike. And while Grant appeared to be dutifully following Washington's two-term precedent when he declined to run in year eight of his presidency, his open desire to run four years later opened up an unlikely new battlefront pitting the former general against an unwritten eighty-four-year-old precedent whose support was wider than it seemed at first.

What had once appeared to be a relatively clear path for Grant to the 1880 Republican nomination had suddenly transformed into an up-hill battle. If Grant and his followers hoped that the four-year period between terms would undercut claims that he was in violation of the tradition, they were mistaken. As the Springer resolution made clear, concerns about Grant's returning to office were considerable once one got beyond some tight-knit Republican party circles. The first warning signs came from John Russell Young, a journalist for the *New York Herald* who had a far greater feel for where the country stood than any of Grant's other advisors. Young had accompanied Grant on his world tour and had impressed the ex-President with his connections in China and elsewhere. Yet by early 1880, Young was convinced Grant could not win a general election, and he told him so that spring.[27] Undaunted, Grant would not give up the fight so easily.

On June 7, 1880, the second-to-last day of the convention, delegates submitted their first ballot for the presidential nomination. With hostility to an unprecedented third term a live issue in the hall, Grant quickly surmised that he was in trouble: while he led all other candidates with 304 votes, he fell 75 votes short of what he needed to clinch the nomination, with little prospect of winning more. Though backed by many of the party bosses, Grant's bid for the nomination immediately stalled thereafter; opponents of Grant led by James G. Blaine and John Sherman found themselves leaders of a growing movement that coalesced in its opposition to the very concept of a third term. The desperation of many Republican delegates to avoid a general election rebuke was also evident at the time: in ballot after ballot, the delegates refused to cast their votes for Grant and eventually turned their attention to compromise possibilities like Benjamin Harrison of Indiana and the eventual victor on the thirty-sixth ballot, Congressman James A. Garfield. The ex-president who had been "received with grand ceremony by monarchs and prime ministers around the world" could not even defeat these two, relatively obscure candidates. Supporters hoped the two previous terms of Grant would buttress his candidacy. In fact, they had helped to defeat him.

In 1880, there were other factors at work against Grant. In a general election, Democrats would be certain to raise the many scandals that arose during his administration. No amount of loyalty to the former union general could wipe away that stain—the former president was at a minimum guilty of extreme dereliction. Additionally, Grant's connections to Conkling and the Stalwarts—which at first created interest in his candidacy from one side of the party–precluded him from selling himself as a compromise choice among the competing factions. At the convention, when state delegations such as Maine finally deserted Blaine, they could not then go to Grant; rather, they looked for a third alternative such as Harrison or Garfield. Finally, Grant's forces clearly underestimated the impact of the delegates' defeat of the "unit rule" early in the convention. Led by Conklin, Grant's supporters lobbied hard for this rule, which would have guaranteed that three of the largest states under Stalwart control (New York, Illinois and Pennsylvania) cast all their votes in unison.[28] When the rule was defeated by a clear 449–306 vote, Grant's chances for the nomination diminished considerably.

None of those factors alone dealt a definitive blow to Grant's chances. With the Democrats already assured of the southern states' electoral votes, the election was likely to be decided in the swing states of New York, Ohio, and Indiana. Desperate to defeat Democrats in the fall, all this internal strife might have been pushed aside had Grant's path not been blocked by the specter of George Washington and the two-term precedent. While many of Washington's contributions would eventually be discarded in favor of new and more modern political traditions and routines, the two-term precedent had become even more engrained in the political culture once eighty-four years passed without a serious attempt at a third term by Jefferson, Monroe, Jackson or anyone else. And in what was shaping up to be a close general election, the reasons why the Stalwarts had turned to Grant would not hold much weight among the general public.

Historians suggest that had Grant served exactly one term in office, he might have been considered one of the greatest presidents in American history by historical standards.[29] That second term—so associated with corruption charges—brought him down several notches and sullied his reputation for competence and effectiveness. Even if Republican leaders were prepared to run the Grant presidency back for a third try, the legacy of George Washington and his two-term precedent made that prospect difficult, if not impossible.

After Grant's failed bid in 1880, the next threat to Washington's precedent came in the form of Grover Cleveland, who won the White House in 1884, lost his reelection bid in 1888, and then recaptured the presidency again in 1892. Would President Cleveland now seek a fourth consecutive Democratic presidential nomination (and an unprecedented third term in the White House) in 1896? No one could doubt Cleveland's resilience, but his second term was marked by extended conflict between him and his party over how to address the acute economic depression that arose from the Panic of 1893. The president had pushed for a repeal of silver coinage as a way of offsetting a national shortage of gold; while moderates rallied to his side, a growing number of "silverites" had seized control of the Democratic Party by the end of Cleveland's second term. Given their strong repudiation of Cleveland and the gold standard, the president's prospects for capturing a fourth straight Democratic nomination were remote at best. The party thus cast its lot against Cleveland's economic policies and in favor of William Jennings Bryan and his silver platform for the next decade until the conservative wing (which included Cleveland) wrestled back control of the party in 1904.

Other factors were also working against Cleveland remaining as president for an additional term. In 1893, Cleveland was forced to undergo surgery to remove a non-malignant tumor in his mouth. Though he would still be just 59 years during the 1896 presidential election, close associates must have wondered if he was up for the job health-wise. In 1894, the Pullman strike over railroad workers' low wages paralyzed the nation's economy and led to charges of Democratic incompetence. Moreover, the 1894 midterm elections had resulted in a Republican landslide, and many anticipated Republican momentum in the 1896 campaign for the White House. Thus, in the highly unlikely case of a Cleveland nomination, his chances of winning a third term seemed long indeed. If Cleveland wanted to embrace retirement enthusiastically, he was stopped only by the reality that he had no hand-picked successor waiting in the wings. Without such an heir available, the president worried and deliberated with political allies, but "did nothing to rally his supporters behind an alternative to [Bryan] as his party's nominee."[30]

To successfully buck the two-term precedent, a president would need political winds at his back and widespread support within his own party; if the president's natural constituency appeared divided on the question, the opposition would be able to gain considerable traction in a general election arguing that the president's bid for a third term was a threat to the separation of powers, or worse.

Unlike Grant and Cleveland, Theodore Roosevelt had the wind at his back as his presidency reached its conclusion in 1908. Roosevelt—who first took office in September 1901 after President William McKinley's assassination and then won election to the White House in his own right in 1904—was in a strong position to become the first president to serve a third distinct term as the nation's president. Having become (at age 42) the youngest man ever to hold the presidency, he was just fifty years old at the time of the 1908 general election. His reputation for living a "strenuous life" through regular exercise including boxing, tennis, horseback riding and even jujitsu left little doubt that he had the stamina to take on a third term. Moreover, his second term in office had been free of the type of catastrophes that doom a president's chances for reelection, and his easy victory in 1904 (with 56 percent of the vote and an electoral margin of 336–140) gave him a considerable working margin at the outset. Finally, Theodore Roosevelt possessed an argument that his two-term predecessors all lacked: unlike them, he had only run for election as president once before, having served out the bulk of McKinley's second term in the White House. Thus, another presidential bid for Roosevelt would at least be consistent with Washington's reluctance to campaign for a third straight term as president.

That left Theodore Roosevelt in the strongest position of any chief executive since Monroe to take on Washington's precedent. Amazingly, it was TR himself who did the most to undermine his long-term political fortunes and transform a near certain third term as president into an uphill climb, even under the best of circumstances. On November 8, 1904, barely minutes after he learned that he had secured election as president for another term, Roosevelt stunned family and associates alike when he declared to the press that he would under no conditions stand as a candidate four years later. The announcement rendered Roosevelt a lame duck from the outset of his second term; regardless, he never once backed away from that promise either publicly or privately. As proof of Roosevelt's continued hold on his party, Secretary of War William Howard Taft was Roosevelt's choice for a successor, and his subsequent election as president gave TR little reason to look back. At least not until four years later, when Roosevelt's bid to return to the White House was blocked in both the summer and fall by the presence of Taft. Even Theodore Roosevelt could not wrestle the Republican nomination away from a sitting president, and as popular as he remained in some circles, he could only play spoiler in the 1912 election, splitting the Republican vote with his onetime ally. Roosevelt thus fell into the same trap as Grant, unable to marshal all the forces of his own political party in favor of a third term. Given how long the two-term precedent had held to that point, his failure to unify the party behind his candidacy was no small matter.

Eight years after Roosevelt's unsuccessful third-party bid, President Woodrow Wilson launched his own assault on Washington's precedent. Wilson was the first Democrat to win a second consecutive term as president since Andrew Jackson, and he had mulled a possible third-term run starting in June 1919. After the Senate rejected US involvement in Wilson's cherished League of Nations in November of 1919, he revived the idea of a possible third term, actively pressing for his candidacy despite continued health concerns arising out of a severe stroke that had left him temporarily incapacitated the previous fall. According to Wilson's biographer,

> That the whole idea was tragically absurd became obvious to members of the Cabinet on April 13 during the first Cabinet meeting with the president since his stroke. His face sagged and he could not stand without assistance, but most serious, he could not follow the discussion of issues in the meeting.[31]

Undaunted, Wilson asked Secretary of State Bainbridge Colby to formally place his name into nomination when the Democratic national convention was held that summer in San Francisco. Wilson's hopes then suffered their most serious blow when his primary physician—who had agreed to hide the severity of Wilson's stroke from government leaders the previous fall—refused to play a part in advancing Wilson's candidacy. Dr. Cary Grayson had urged Wilson to resign earlier that summer; when he refused, he met with party leaders and implored them to "save the life of this great man."[32]

Colby remained a stalwart Wilson supporter even as the president suffered from his stroke in late 1919 and early 1920. And if Colby had been named permanent chairman of the convention (as Wilson intended), he might even have succeeded in moving President Wilson's name forward. But Grayson's revelations convinced Democratic Party leaders that the president's health could not withstand the rigors of another campaign and that the "very attempt to nominate him would only serve to embarrass him."[33] The convention was ready for a new standard-bearer anyway: a majority of the delegates were supportive of Wilson's policies, but not his candidacy. For his part, Colby saw the writing on the wall, and he never formally nominated Wilson. After days of negotiations and numerous ballots, the convention nominated the ticket of Ohio Governor James Cox and Assistant Secretary of the Navy Franklin Delano Roosevelt. That ticket was overwhelmingly defeated by the Republicans in November of 1920.

Three years later, Vice President Calvin Coolidge stepped in to fill the term of yet another president (Warren Harding) who died in office. Like Theodore Roosevelt two decades earlier, Coolidge subsequently won election to the White House in his own right. Coolidge also followed Roosevelt's lead in taking himself out of consideration for a second presidential campaign, though he waited much longer to issue his proclamation: while vacationing in the Black Hills of South Dakota during the summer of 1928, Coolidge announced that he "would not seek a second full term as president." The outcome was the same for both Republican presidents: each man forfeited the opportunity to run for reelection under advantageous political conditions.

Why did Coolidge refuse to throw his hat into the 1928 race? Personal concerns were clearly a factor, as his wife Grace Coolidge had been in bad health since the summer of 1927.[34] Those close to Coolidge believed the novelty of being president had worn off of Coolidge as well, and as there was no great national crisis during his second term, there was little need for a continuation of the current White House leadership.[35] When Commerce Secretary Herbert Hoover visited Coolidge in September of 1927, he was resigned to support a Coolidge candidacy if the president wanted to keep his job. Instead, Coolidge's cryptic response to Hoover's inquiry told him all he needed to know: Reportedly, Coolidge may have indicated to his secretary that ten years in office was "too long for a president in this country."[36] Still, Coolidge was never intimidated by the prospect of becoming the first president to serve longer than Washington. Rather, he did not want the job any longer and he could not bring himself to state otherwise, even if doing so in 1927 would have allowed him to at least keep his options open the following year. In this one respect, Coolidge proved that he was nothing like Theodore Roosevelt, who recognized the gravity of his error when he departed the White House for good in March of 1909.

Franklin Delano Roosevelt Breaks Through

Had Washington's two-term precedent lost its resilience by 1940, when Franklin Roosevelt and the Democrats chose to defy it? In truth, there was nothing inevitable about FDR's decision to run for an unprecedented third term in office. Like many presidents before him, Franklin Roosevelt rejected the idea of another run early in the election year of 1940. His decision, though expressed only privately, appeared both genuine and permanent. Consistent with that judgment, Roosevelt signed a contract in January of that year for $75,000 annually to serve as a contributing editor at *Colliers* magazine, providing twenty-six articles a year for three years after he left the White House in 1941. The president then did the rounds with the most ambitious members of his administration: He informed Secretary of State Cordell Hull, Postmaster General James Farley and others that he was excited to retire. Privately, he urged each of them to seek the Democratic nomination on their own.[37] To select supporters who pleaded with him to run again, he left little doubt of his intentions. On one occasion he told Teamsters president Daniel Tobin that he was "tired . . . I really am. I can't be president again."[38] If FDR was indeed planning to leave, these actions were advisable, if not technically required.

Changing circumstances over the next seven months did not merely open up an unexpected pathway to Roosevelt's third term as president; by the summer of 1940, opposition to FDR's candidacy among the Democratic faithful would have seemed downright unpatriotic. The first key development that altered the political calculus was the Nazi blitzkrieg that captured France in May of that year. As the German army advanced through Europe against only token resistance, Roosevelt was discouraged by party officials from formally withdrawing his name from the race; declaring himself a lame duck would have hampered his ability to influence events abroad, and in particular, it would have strained communications with Great Britain. Roosevelt now had some room to backtrack on some of these earlier signals.

FDR himself later recounted for supporters how these events around the world moved him to postpone short-term political considerations in favor of a greater cause:

> Swiftly moving foreign events made necessary swift action at home and beyond the seas. Plans for national defense had to be expanded and adjusted to meet new forms of warfare. American citizens and their welfare had to be safeguarded in many foreign zones of danger. National unity in the United States became a crying essential in the face of the development of unbelievable types of espionage and international treachery. Every day that passed called for the postponement of personal plans and partisan debate until the latest possible moment.[39]

The second of the Democrats' political considerations was related to the first: the need for a unified party during an international crisis. On this point everyone agreed: the president offered the best hope of achieving such unity. If the Republicans nominated an isolationist or outspoken opponent of the New Deal, the GOP could effectively frame the 1940 election as a referendum on Roosevelt's policies. Without Roosevelt on the ticket, it would be more difficult (though by no means impossible) to defend them. FDR was better equipped to parry attacks on the New Deal than anyone else, as no one knew those policies and decisions better than him. On the other hand, if the Republicans nominated a candidate who accepted FDR's overall approach in domestic and foreign policy, Roosevelt would be the only Democratic candidate who could offer a sharp choice, as any other Democrat would take the same general position as the Republican. Why trust America to "Roosevelt lite" when you could have the real thing? Democratic bosses in nearly every state started to line up their organizations in favor of a third Roosevelt term.

It was the latter scenario that eventually emerged. At their June 1940 convention in Philadelphia, the Republicans turned to a dark horse: the charismatic Wall Street-based industrialist Wendell Willkie. Here was a Republican who supported most of Roosevelt's social programs and was an outspoken advocate of Great Britain in its war against the Nazis. The GOP thought Willkie could beat any Democratic candidate other than Roosevelt. In this one instance, Washington's two-term precedent had an unusual influence on the proceedings, as the Republican party assumed FDR would follow in the footsteps of Jefferson, Madison, and everyone else and forego yet another term as president.

The traditional order of the conventions (incumbent party second) now worked in Roosevelt's favor, as did the unusually long three-week gap between the two conventions. During that period extending from June 28 until July 15, 1940, support for a third Roosevelt term gathered steady momentum in response to the Willkie gambit. Still, nothing was inevitable in the pursuit of an unprecedented third term in office: Following the two conventions, an August Gallup poll found FDR and Willkie in a virtual dead heat. Then in September, as the Battle of Britain was waged in the skies over London, the Democrats' predictions proved correct, as Willkie felt compelled to articulate a starker choice for the voters. Specifically, he attacked Roosevelt for secretly dragging the United States into war. Roosevelt responded with the clever declaration that he would "not send American boys into any *foreign wars*." Who would fault a president for fighting a war that came to American shores? Suddenly, Willkie was unable to move the needle, and the continued reports from Europe only argued further for Roosevelt's experience and sure handedness. In the November election, FDR won 55 percent of the popular vote, including 38 of the 48 states. The two-term precedent had finally been punctured, as Roosevelt became the only man in American history to take the oath of office for a third time on January 20, 1941.[40]

At least five different (though related) factors combined to propel FDR's candidacy forward in 1940. If any of those circumstances had been different, the two-term precedent might have offered a far more daunting obstacle for FDR and the Democrats. First, a relatively popular president continued to enjoy a clear majority of the public's support.[41] This was not the case with Grant, Wilson, or Cleveland, each of whom faced the reality of declining popularity during their respective second terms. Second, the Democratic Party lacked any clear alternative candidates waiting in the wings to challenge FDR. Third, the breakout of war in Europe placed a premium on the presence of experienced leadership in the White House. The argument for "new blood" and a "fresh approach" would have been received quite differently absent an international crisis of this magnitude.

Fourth, FDR's maneuvering around the two-term precedent proved masterful. Rather than argue there was no precedent or confronting its logic head on, FDR offered a more deferential approach. When he was specifically challenged publicly about his willingness to defy Washington's example, FDR dismissed the possibility as unlikely, while never actually encouraging other candidates to step forward. He could afford this approach because, as noted above, there were no strong candidates waiting in the wings. Unlike Jefferson (who had Madison) or his cousin Theodore (who had been grooming Taft), there was no hand-chosen successor—nor would one ever emerge. Finally, Republican Party bosses gambled that FDR would not run, and thus nominated a dark horse candidate in Willkie. As it turns out, Willkie's lack of political experience only served to highlight Roosevelt's strengths as an experienced and weathered leader. Add to all these factors the presence of Eleanor Roosevelt, who later backtracked on her opposition to a third term and even agreed to address the Democratic convention on her husband's behalf. FDR could not have scripted a more fortuitous set of circumstances for his third-term candidacy.

In truth, Willkie was capable of defeating any Democratic candidate other than Roosevelt,[42] and he ran a spirited campaign under the most trying of circumstances. Willkie might have benefitted from comparisons with President Roosevelt on the campaign trail, where his relative youth and vigor (he was just 48 years old) offered a stark contrast with a president who was ten years older and suffered from a disability. Yet when FDR declared that he would not actively campaign "because of the world crisis," Willkie lost even that advantage. Of course, an even bigger problem was the growing international crisis, which left Willkie without a cause. Though he opposed sending armaments to Britain without Congressional authorization, the former Democrat was not an isolationist and thus generated little enthusiasm among conservatives in the party. The third-term issue simply fizzled under these circumstances.[43] New York City's independent mayor Fiorella LaGuardia summed up the 1940 election in a nutshell: Given the lack of stark differences, "I would rather have FDR with all his known faults than Willkie with his unknown qualities."[44]

It might be tempting to see FDR's 1940 presidential bid as the final nail in the coffin of a precedent that was never formally binding in the first place. There was no magical significance to the amount of two terms anyway; Washington believed in a voluntary exit . . . whenever that might take place. And yet any fair reading of the events that transpired in 1940 creates a far different impression: that it took such an unlikely series of developments to give FDR that third consecutive term, which only proves just how imposing a precedent it had actually become. Whether or not the two-term precedent was established in writing did not matter: it was engraved in the American psyche. Before 1940, ten different presidents had served all or part of two terms in office and every one of them peacefully handed over power to a successor. The American public had every reason to believe 1940 would follow the same pattern. It took a military assault on America's European allies to knock over the two-term wall that Washington created 144 years earlier.

The 22nd Amendment and the Politics of Wishful Thinking

Franklin Delano Roosevelt served as president of the United States for the final twelve years of his life. He suffered an intracerebral hemorrhage and died on the afternoon of April 12, 1945, at the age of 63. It was the type of exit that George Washington had most feared for himself and his successors; FDR remained in office until he was well past his physical and mental primes. Indeed, FDR's health had been a frequent subject of speculation starting in 1942, if not earlier. During the 1944 election contest, Roosevelt's doctors were forced to deny his health was poor on multiple occasions. These denials helped him survive his closest presidential election contest, but few expected he would survive an entire fourth term in office.

FDR's route to the White House had seemed predestined: Not even his bout with polio in the 1920s could upset his progress along a well-trodden political pathway that included service at the top levels of the naval department, his party's nomination to the vice presidency, and eventually a stint as governor of New York. His cousin Theodore had made all those same stops as well. The New York state governorship in particular had become the most popular venue for grooming future presidential nominees, including Van Buren, Tilden, Cleveland, Hughes, Al Smith, and two different Roosevelts.

By contrast, Harry S. Truman's rise to the presidency was hardly preordained: He rose to the US senate on the strength of the Prendergast political machine back in Missouri, and then captured his party's vice-presidential nomination in 1944 as the last man standing when Henry Wallace, William O. Douglas, and the other possibilities proved objectionable to the Democratic party bosses. No one could have guessed that like FDR, Truman himself would eventually confront Washington's two-term precedent as well as he weighed whether to run again for president in 1952.

Unlike FDR, Truman had become exceedingly unpopular by the end of his presidency; after winning a nailbiter election contest against Thomas Dewey in 1948, the second term of his unlikely presidency began to resemble Grant's, as the US Senate investigated charges of corruption that had been leveled against many senior officials in his administration. Senator Joseph McCarthy's anti-communist crusade dovetailed nicely onto those corruption charges, as he stoked fears that the Soviet Union had infiltrated many of those same bureaucracies. Though President Truman himself tried to respond with proposed reforms to the Internal Revenue Bureau (later the IRS) and other troubled agencies, corruption was likely to become a major issue in any 1952 election campaign.

In considering his prospects for a third term in office, President Truman also had to deal with the reality that Congress (and perhaps the country as a whole) had made its own peace with FDR's decision to challenge Washington's unwritten two-term precedent. The Republican party platforms of 1940 and 1944 had responded to FDR's potential candidacy by calling for a constitutional amendment imposing term limits. Right after FDR's passing, a substantial number of Democratic legislators led by Senator Warren Magnuson (D-WA.) joined in that initiative as well. Suddenly, presidential term limits had become a bipartisan cause. The invocation of Washington's two-term tradition helped negate the partisan nature of the amendment as well.

Thus, beginning in 1947, Congress moved to prevent future presidents from relying on FDR as their new working precedent. It did so by proposing a constitutional amendment which provided that (1) no one who has been elected president twice may be elected again; and (2) anyone who fills an unexpired presidential term lasting more than two years is prohibited from being elected president more than once. If this amendment had been in place at the turn of the century, it would have prevented Theodore Roosevelt from seeking the presidency again in 1908 (when he declined to run) or in 1912 (when he ran as a third-party candidate). And while the terms of the proposal included a grandfather clause exempting President Truman (the article would "not apply to any person [then] holding the office of the president"), the message of the amendment was clear: Washington's unwritten two-term precedent would soon become part of the Constitution itself. If President Truman did run for president again in 1952, he would be running against a political culture that now formally frowned on that very act.

As predicted, the Twenty-second Amendment to the Constitution was ratified in less than four years' time. The House of Representatives approved the amendment on February 6, 1947, by a 285-121 vote with 47 Democrats in favor; the Senate followed suit with revisions by a 59-23 vote (with 16 Democrats in favor) on March 12, 1947. The House then agreed to the Senate's revisions on March 21, the day the Congress sent it to the states for ratification.

The final language of the amendment read as follows:

Section 1. No person shall be elected to the office of the President more than twice, and no person who has held the office of President, or acted as President, for more than two years of a term to which some other person was elected President shall be elected to the office of the President more than once. But this Article shall not apply to any person holding the office of President when this Article was proposed by the Congress, and shall not prevent any person who may be holding the office of President, or acting as President, during the term within which this Article becomes operative from holding the office of President or acting as President during the remainder of such term.

Section 2. This Article shall be inoperative unless it shall have been ratified as an amendment to the Constitution by the legislatures of three-fourths of the several states within seven years from the date of its submission to the states by the Congress.

The 22nd Amendment became part of the Constitution just four years later when it was ratified by the Minnesota legislature (the 36th of 48 states) on February 27, 1951. Five more states voted to ratify after Minnesota, giving the amendment a final tally of 41 out of 48 states.

The amendment's relatively swift ratification offers further testament to Washington's lasting influence over the American political system. That it occurred so soon after Roosevelt's passing—and with a degree of bipartisan support—is also telling. And while five states neglected to act on the amendment, only two (Oklahoma and Massachusetts) outright rejected it.

Even after the amendment was ratified, President Truman took steps toward running for a third term of his own. Yet by early 1952, the president sported very weak polling numbers: Gallup placed his approval at 22 percent on February 14, 1952.[45] Among likely Democratic voters, Truman was not doing much better. A poll taken weeks before the New Hampshire primary in March gave President Truman just 36 percent support. While this placed him ahead of contenders such as Senators Ernest Kefauver of Tennessee (21 percent) as well as his own vice president, Alben Barkley (17 percent), it was a discouraging sign for a sitting president. Moreover, the president's prospects for gaining support during the spring appeared quite limited. With the Korean War continuing to rage and his approval rating plummeting, those February polling numbers represented the high-water mark of Truman's primary support.

On March 11, 1952, Senator Kefauver handed the president a stunning defeat in the New Hampshire primary, winning 19,800 votes (almost 4,000 more than Truman) and securing all eight delegates at stake. Truman's bid for a third term was effectively over: Within days he formally withdrew his name from consideration in any future primaries. Years later, the president would attempt to frame the decision as unrelated to any specific primary results. That would be a gratuitous reading to be sure. This much is true: President Truman retired from office short of making a formal and sustained run for a third term as president even though the law at the time allowed him to do so.

In the final analysis, the Twenty-second amendment hardly represented a sea change in how American politics would be conducted going forward. Resistance to presidential service beyond two terms in office was already a core pillar of the American political culture; the amendment was primarily intended to embed Washington's example into the Constitution, in case a future president ever found himself in the unlikely set of circumstances that had made Franklin Roosevelt's third and fourth terms possible.

In modern times, the mere presence of the Twenty-second Amendment, combined with a healthy American skepticism of chief executives who hold power too long—have removed from modern presidents any hope that they might stay in the White House indefinitely. Until 1951, Washington's decision was the primary factor influencing numerous presidents who followed him to choose retirement. Without that long tradition in place, FDR's four successive election victories would not have seemed so aberrational; nor would calls for the Twenty-second Amendment have seemed so compelling. And perhaps the republic we live in today would be a fundamentally different place as well.

Conclusion

Looking Back And Looking Ahead

"Reluctant heroes gain fame throughout history by denying the path of despotism . . . the denial of power that actually increases one's power is a dynamic that possesses a long history."

Michael J. Hillyard

During his unsuccessful campaign for reelection in 2020, Donald Trump would often speculate to crowds not just about a potential second term in office, but about a possible third term as well. "We are going to win four more years," Trump told supporters at one rally in Oshkosh, Wisconsin, "and then after that, we'll go for another four years because they spied on my campaign. We should get a redo!"[1] Joseph Biden's victory in the general election that November rendered talk of Trump's staying in office beyond a second term moot, at least for the time being. In retrospect, it might seem amazing to some that an American politician could even joke about such a scenario, as the clear words of the Twenty-second Amendment block the possibility of an individual being elected president for a third time, or otherwise serving beyond two-and-a-half terms.

President Trump's rhetoric offers a reminder to us as well—that nothing in American politics is impossible. Written laws have never provided an impenetrable obstacle when public officials want something desperately enough and the public is either willing to go along or unwilling to stand in the way. Statutes can be reinterpreted or altered, and even specific constitutional language can be overcome, if not outright ignored. The Twelfth Amendment revised our Article II election procedures; the Sixteenth Amendment overturned constitutional language that prohibited taxes not apportioned among the states in proportion to their representation; and the Twenty-first Amendment outright repealed the Eighteenth Amendment which had established Prohibition. The impossible is never so impossible as we might suppose.

Consider the assumed inviolability of term limits that apply to high-level officials. Leaders of other countries have found ways to circumvent similar provisions that appear to limit them from continually staying in power. In modern times, both Russian president Vladimir Putin and Chinese president Xi Jinping have changed or removed term limits. Executives in countries as diverse as Azerbaijan, Bolivia and Iraq have done the same. Politicians in the United States are not above engaging in such strategic maneuvers themselves, as they have taken action to cast aside term limits that were laid out explicitly. As recently as in 2008, Mayor Michael Bloomberg convinced New York City's council to modify its own term limits law, allowing him to run (and win) a third consecutive term beginning on January 1, 2010.

Of course, the modification of local statutory law is one thing; amending the federal constitution is quite another. In American history there have only been just twenty-seven formal amendments to the Constitution, with eleven of those passing during the first five years of the nation's existence. Yet it remains the case that the US Constitution has survived mostly intact precisely because most of its provisions are not nearly so limiting as they might seem. In fact, American presidents have often acted in the face of constitutional language that appeared otherwise restrictive. James K. Polk ordered the US army to occupy territory claimed by New Mexico without a Congressional declaration of war; Abraham Lincoln suspended habeas corpus requirements for prisoners during the Civil War. More recently, Donald Trump diverted money from the Department of Defense budget to build a border wall without Congressional approval; he also appeared to ignore the Constitution's emoluments clause, which on its face required him to give up ownership and control of his sprawling business empire while serving as president. In all these cases and others, neither impeachment nor the judicial process presented much of a deterrent to stop such initiatives in the hands of determined chief executives. Sometimes federal law or constitutional amendments are passed (or ratified) to justify those actions after the fact. Sometimes they never receive any such retroactive validation.

Still, might the extension of a president's term of service be a bridge too far, given the centrality those provisions play in holding chief executives accountable under our constitution? Even a norm-busting executive like Donald Trump would face untold resistance if he tried to circumvent the clear language of the Twenty-second Amendment (aspiring presidents within his own Republican party might see to that in pursuit of their own interests). And yet the issue continues to arise, perhaps because like many other political leaders, most presidents want to stay in power as long as possible. As Bertrand Russell famously opined, power is a drug whose desire only tends to increase with "the habit of responsibility."[2] One can grow accustomed to the perks of office without even realizing it; and while the job is a significant burden for many, few presidents leave office with absolute confidence that their legacy is secure or that their successor will do any better.

The bottom line is that in the examples above, James K. Polk and Abraham Lincoln were not forced to confront a precedent established by that most untouchable of icons, George Washington. Until the Twenty-second Amendment was ratified in 1951, presidential term limits were not formally established as a matter of law. They were informally established only to the degree that George Washington felt like two terms was enough for him; subsequent presidents for the most part followed his lead up until Franklin Delano Roosevelt's election to a third term in November of 1940. In a similar vein, the peaceful rotation of officeholders persisted for so long in part because George Washington gave the principle his support in 1796. The first president was committed to the principle of an emboldened and effective executive . . . but one who *did not seek to stay in power as long as possible*. As the inaugural president of the Society of the Cincinnati, he was more than comfortable invoking the spirit of Lucius Quinctius Cincinnatus, who voluntarily ceded power to others after serving as consul and then dictator of Rome.

During the 154-year period between George Washington's departure from the political scene and ratification of the Twenty-second Amendment, thirteen presidents served all or part of two separate presidential terms, and only one of those thirteen individuals successfully served in a third term as well. Sometimes the president decided for himself that two terms were enough. Sometimes the political system pushed back against the two-term president's efforts to secure a longer presidency. Regardless, no actual legal restriction stood in their way—just George

Washington and the example he set. When the dam finally broke in 1940, the political system acted in a bipartisan fashion to build it back up in the form of the Twenty-second Amendment. Credit for that development as well must go largely to George Washington and the political culture he created.

All this makes it even more important that we seek to understand George Washington's decision to leave the White House of his own accord after two terms in office. The pressures on the first president to seek a third term in 1796 were enormous. Many of the same forces that had called for his reelection in 1792 were calling for him to continue (albeit with far less enthusiasm in the case of Thomas Jefferson and James Madison). Though Vice President John Adams regarded himself as Washington's heir apparent, the Federalists were far from united in their belief that he should become the nation's second president. Dark clouds hovered over the new nation in foreign policy, endangering many of the gains made during Washington's two terms in office. Who but Washington would be able to ensure that the US maintained its neutrality? And while Washington's health was suspect, it had always been so. Mount Vernon was in economic turmoil, but that had been the case for the better part of two decades. Most presidents in his position would have sought a third term and never looked back.

Of the many considerations that went into Washington's political calculus in 1796, one appears to stand out above the rest. The first president of the United States was deeply concerned about his personal and political legacy. Up until 1796, he was able to pursue a path that promoted the interests of the nation in general and the institution of the presidency in particular. He had allowed the long-term concerns of the nation to overwhelm short-term personal considerations at every turn, because his long-term personal interests (his legacy of civic virtue and selflessness) would remain intact. Whereas many politicians pursue immediate rewards and victories while remaining confident that the long-term would eventually bend to their will, George Washington seemed to instinctively know better. By 1796, Washington understood that if he stepped down, his presidency would be remembered not so much for its accomplishments, as for its devotion to republicanism and civic virtue.

Accordingly, Washington's parting gift to the nation was a novel one: that he would voluntarily depart. He did not intend to create a specific two-term precedent that applied under all circumstances to every one of his successors. That meant future presidents could theoretically argue that Washington's precedent was not a form of advocacy against serving more than two terms. No president is indispensable or irreplaceable . . . not even George Washington. Some would leave after one term; others after two; and on exceedingly rare occasions, perhaps after three or four. If Washington had chosen to stay beyond March of 1797, he would have sent the opposite message to the country as well as those who might be in his own position someday.

Like Washington twelve years earlier, Thomas Jefferson stepped down after two terms of his office. But was this step really so magnanimous and consistent with the principle of rotation? As president, Jefferson wrote to the legislature of Vermont in 1807:

> Believing that a representative government, responsible at short periods of election, is that which produces the greatest sum of happiness to mankind, I feel it a duty to do no act which shall essentially impair that principle; and I should unwillingly be the person who, disregarding the sound precedent set by an illustrious predecessor, should furnish the first example of prolongation beyond the second term of office.[3]

Jefferson faced quite different circumstances than Washington when he departed after just two terms, which made his exit seem less voluntary by comparison. His second term in office had not gone as well as his first, and unlike Washington, he actively groomed a like-minded successor in the form of Secretary of State James Madison. Washington's departure in 1796 encouraged Jefferson and others to leave after just two terms when they would not have done so otherwise. Non-judicial, unwritten precedents are never so clear or unambiguous, but their impact may still be felt in profound and lasting ways. Notwithstanding ratification of the Twenty-second Amendment, more tests of this principle will come in the years ahead. Presidents will continue to struggle to overcome the two-term precedent, just as they have done in the past.

NOTES

PREFACE AND ACKNOWLEDGMENTS

1. In his book *The Hardest Job in the World: The American Presidency* (New York: Random House, 2020), journalist and commentator John Dickerson of CBS News argues that in addition to managing an office with an "ever-expanding job description," the emotional burdens of the presidency are "unfathomable."

2. Irvin Molotsky, "Reagan Wants End of Two-Term Limit," *New York Times*, November 29, 1987, (https://www.nytimes.com/1987/11/29/us/reagan-wants-end-of-two-term-limit.html).

3. Martin Kettle, "Clinton Wants Third Term in Office," *Guardian*, December 7, 2000, (https://www.theguardian.com/world/2000/dec/08/uselections2000.usa3).

4. Alexandra Del Rosario, "Barack Obama Explains to Stephen Colbert the Satisfaction of Being President, What A Third Term Could Have Looked Like," *Deadline*, November 30, 2020 (https://deadline.com/2020/11/barack-obama-stephen-colbert-president-third-term-1234635491/).

5. Ronald Reagan finished his presidency with his approval rating above 60 percent; Bill Clinton left the White House with his approval rating hovering near 66 percent; and Barack Obama's rating stood at 59 percent in January of 2017.

6. Joseph Ellis, *American Dialogue: The Founding Fathers and Us* (New York: Alfred Knopf, 2018), 174.

7. Though resistance to the new tax continued after the rebellion was finally put down in 1794, all the rebels were either acquitted or pardoned.

8. In fact, Washington took office on April 30, 1789, and served several weeks short of eight years when he departed office on March 4, 1797, the day designated by Congress as the start of the next term.

9. See John Dickerson, "The Hardest Job in the World: What If the Problem Isn't the President—It's the Presidency?" *Atlantic*, May 2018 (https://www.theatlantic.com/magazine/archive/2018/05/a-broken-office/556883/).

INTRODUCTION: GEORGE WASHINGTON AND THE TWO-TERM PRECEDENT

1. In this instance I distinguish what the Confederate States of America did in 1861 (seeking by violent means to secede from the United States and form their own independent nation) from the events of January 6, 2021, when a mob sought to disrupt the counting of Electoral College votes and thereby overturn President Donald Trump's defeat in the November 2020 presidential election. The latter events were aimed at taking over the current government, rather than forming a new one.

2. Adam Przeworski, "Acquiring the Habit of Changing Governments Through Elections," *Comparative Political Studies* 48, vol. 1 (2015), 101–129.

3. The details of that day's proceedings can be found in John E. Ferling, *The First of Men: A Life of George Washington* (New York: Oxford University Press, 1988), 484.

4. Even John Adams' own wife Abigail had doubts as to whether her husband could "fill Washington's place" as leader of the new nation. See Jonathan Horn, *Washington's End: The Final Years and Forgotten Struggle* (New York: Simon & Schuster, 2020), 2.

5. Willard Sterne Randall, *George Washington: A Life* (New York: Henry Holt, 1997), p. 493.

6. Inaugural Address of John Adams, March 4, 1797 (https://avalon.law.yale.edu/18th_century/adams.asp) (emphasis added).

7. According to Ron Chernow, Adams surmised that Washington had retired because "a malign Hamilton wielded veto power over his appointees," though later he offered a more objective opinion: "The times were critical, the labor fatiguing, many circumstances disgusting and he felt weary and longed for retirement." Chernow, *Washington: A Life* (New York: Penguin Books, 2010), 757.

8. In a letter to his wife penned the following day, Adams recounted the quick moment he and Washington shared after his address had concluded: "He seemed to enjoy a triumph over me. Me thought I heard him say "AY! I am fairly out and you fairly in! See which of us will be happiest!" See Willard Sterne Randall, *George Washington: A Life,* (New York: Henry Holt & Co., 1997), 493.]

9. In fact, that was how he was eulogized at his funeral just two years later.

10. David Andress, *The Threshold of The Modern Age* (New York: Farrar, Straus & Giroux, 2008) 246.

11. Andress, *Threshold,* 247.

12. James McGregor Burns and Susan Dunn, *George Washington* (New York: Times Books, 2004), 138.

13. John Rhodenhamel, *George Washington: The Wonder of the Age* (New Haven: Yale University Press, 2017), 6.

14. The inflationary issuance of paper currency by both Congress and the states alike harmed the economy, and the weak federal government was unable to adequately provision his army.

15. Contrary to popular misconceptions, Hamilton's birthplace in the British West Indies did not legally prevent him from becoming president. In fact, the Constitution states the president must be either a natural-born citizen or "a citizen of the United States at the time of the Constitution's adoption," which Hamilton clearly was. In fact, the eighth president of the United States, Martin Van Buren (born in 1782), became the first president to qualify for the presidency as a natural-born citizen.

16. After the Jay Treaty was signed in November of 1794, Washington's commitment to neutrality seemed increasingly suspect to Jefferson and Madison.

17. Joseph Ellis, *His Excellency: George Washington* (New York: Vintage Books, 2004), 233.

18. Chernow, *Washington*, 455.

19. Michael Gerhardt, *The Power of Precedent* (New York: Oxford University Press, 2008), 142. Gerhardt discusses the so-called "network effects" of these non-judicial precedents at length. See *Power of Precedent*, 138–145.

20. Gerhardt, *Power of Precedent*, 128.

21. Thomas Jefferson, letter to James Madison, December 20, 1787, in *The Republic of Letters: The Correspondence between Thomas Jefferson and James Madison, 1776–1826*, 3 vols, ed. James Morton Smith (New York: W.W. Norton, 1995), 1:512–514.

22. Thomas Carlyle, *On Heroes, Hero-Worship and the Heroic in History* (1869), repr. New Haven: Yale University Press, 2013).

CHAPTER 1: SACRIFICE (1787–1792)

1. Michael J. Hillyard, *Cincinnatus and the Citizen-Servant Ideal* (New York: Xlibris Corp, 2001), 125.

2. Francois Furstenberg, *In the Name of the Father: Washington's Legacy, Slavery, and The Making of a Nation* (New York: Penguin, 2006), 66.

3. Stephen Howard Browne, *The First Inauguration: George Washington and the Invention of the Republic* (University Park, PA: Penn State University Press, 2020), 15.

4. Dennis Rasmussen, *Fears of a Setting Sun: The Disillusionment of America's Founders* (Princeton, NJ: Princeton University Press, 2021), 23.

5. Center for Digital History, "Hospitality at Mount Vernon," George Washington's Mount Vernon, https://www.mountvernon.org/library/digitalhistory/digital-encyclopedia/article/hospitality-at-mount-vernon/.

6. Rasmussen, *Fears of a Setting Sun*, 21.

7. Daniel Shays was just one of many disgruntled former soldiers who would famously lead an uprising against debt collectors in Massachusetts two years later.

8. Alexis Coe, *You Never Forget Your First: A Biography of George Washington* (New York: Viking, 2020), 51.

9. Coe, *You Never Forget*, 99.

10. According to Joseph Ellis, "the marginal status of [Washington's] farms at Mount Vernon before the war declined further after the war, a condition from which they never recovered ... [b]y the end of the decade he was forced to borrow money and consider the sale of several western parcels to meet his annual expenses." (Ellis, *His Excellency*, 302, n. 35).

11. Joel Achenbach, "George Washington's Western Adventure," *Washington Post*, June 6, 2004, https://www.washingtonpost.com/archive/lifestyle/magazine/2004/06/06/george-washingtons-western-adventure/16ad5da5-388c-481e-8cca-4ef6899a8b92/ (accessed April 5, 2021).

12. Achenbach, "George Washington's Western Adventure."

13. Chernow, *Washington*, 513–514.

14. Rasmussen, *Fears of a Setting Sun*, 21.

15. Robert F. Jones, *George Washington* (New York: Fordham University Press, 1986), 80.

16. Jones, *George Washington*, 80.

17. Andress, *The Threshold*, 41.

18. Jonathan Horn, *Washington's End: The Final Years and Forgotten Struggle* (New York: Simon & Schuster, 2020), 104.

19. Jones, *George Washington*, 159.

20. Jones, *George Washington*, 83.

21. Edward J. Larson, *The Return of George Washington,1783–1789* (New York: HarperCollins, 2014), 133.

22. Browne, *First Inauguration*, 145–146.

23. The provisions of the various state constitutions at the time of the convention are listed in Michael Korzi's book on *Presidential Term Limits in American History*, 24.

24. Korzi, *Presidential Term Limits*, 27.

25. See Max Farrand, *Records of the Federal Convention*, vol. 1, 21 (proceedings of 5/29/1787); vol. 1, 244 (proceedings of 6/15/1787).

26. Farrand, *Records of the Federal Convention*, vol. 1, 74 (proceedings of 6/1/1787).

27. Farrand, *Records of the Federal Convention*, vol. 2, 33 (proceedings of 7/17/1787).

28. Thomas E. Cronin, "Presidential Terms, Tenure, and Re-eligibility," in Thomas E. Cronin, ed., *Inventing the American Presidency* (Lawrence: University Press of Kansas, 1989), 71.

29. Cronin, "Presidential Terms," 71.

30. Cronin, "Presidential Terms," 67.

31. Farrand, *Records of the Federal Convention*, vol. 1, 289 (6/18/1787); Cronin, "Presidential Terms," 66.

32. Noble E. Cunningham, *Jefferson vs. Hamilton: Confrontations that Shaped a Nation* (Boston: Bedford/St. Martin's, 2000), 21

33. Korzi, *Presidential Term Limits*, 29.

34. The committee has at various times also been called the "Committee on Unfinished Parts" as well as the third "Committee of 11," to distinguish it from a first committee of 11 (appointed to draft the full constitution on July 24, 1787) and the second committee of 11 (appointed to consider issues concerning uniform duties and fees on August 25, 1787). Chaired by David Brearly of New Jersey, the other ten members of the Committee of Postponed Parts included Abraham Baldwin (GA), Pierce Butler (SC), Daniel Carrol (MD), John Dickinson (DE), Nicholas Gilman (NH), Rufus King (MA), James Madison (VA), Gouverneur Morris (PA), Roger Sherman (CT), and Hugh Williamson (NC). See generally John R. Vile, "The Critical Role of Committees at the U.S. Constitutional Convention of 1787," *The American Journal of Legal History*, vol. 48, (2006), 148–176.

35. David Stewart, *The Summer of 1787: The Men who Invented the Constitution* (New York: Simon & Schuster, 2008), 209.

36. Cronin, "Presidential Terms," 68.

37. Cronin, "Presidential Terms," 68.

38. John William Perrin, "Presidential Tenure and Re-eligibility," *Political Science Quarterly*, vol. 29, no. 3 (September 1914), 424–425.

39. Their opposition would continue to be heard for several years afterwards, as proposals to change these provisions were raised in Congress in 1789, and then again in 1803 and 1826.

40. Jones, *George Washington*, 83.

41. Jones, *George Washington*, 83.

42. GW, letter to Marquis de Lafayette, April 28, 1788, in Farrand, *Records of the Federal Convention*, vol. 3, 297–298.

43. Thomas Fleming, *The Great Divide: The Conflict Between Washington and Jefferson that Defined a Nation* (Philadelphia: De Capo, 2015), 39.

44. See GW, letter to D. Humphreys, October 10, 1787, in *George Washington, Writings*, ed. John Rhodehamel (New York: Library of America, 1997), 657.

45. Fleming, *Great Divide*, 39.

46. Burns and Dunn, *George Washington*, 128.

47. Andress, *The Threshold*, 247.

48. Browne, *First Inauguration*, 607.

49. Andress, *The Threshold*, 247.

50. Browne, *First Inauguration*, 144.

51. See Thomas Kidd, *Patrick Henry: First Among Patriots* (New York: Basic Books, 2011), 191–192.

52. Hugh Chisolm, ed., "Randolph, Edmund," *Encyclopedia Britannica*, 11th edition, vol. 22 (Cambridge: Cambridge University Press, 1911), 886.

53. Mary Stockwell, "Ratification of the Constitution," George Washington's Mount Vernon https://www.mountvernon.org/library/digitalhistory/digital-encyclopedia/article/ratification-of-the-constitution/ (accessed May 17, 2021).

54. Randall, *George Washington: A Life*, 437.

55. *The Works of Alexander Hamilton*, vol. 1 (New York: C. S. Francis, 1850), 474.

56. Randall, *George Washington*, 437.

57. GW, letter to Henry Knox, April 1, 1789, https://ap.gilderlehrman.org/resource/first-inauguration-george-washington-and-his-reluct?period=3 (accessed May 14, 2021).

58. Ron Chernow, "George Washington: The Reluctant President," *Smithsonian Magazine*, February 2011, https://www.smithsonianmag.com/history/george-washington-the-reluctant-president-49492/.) (accessed May 24, 2021).

59. Chernow, "George Washington: The Reluctant President." According to Edward J. Larson, in 1789, Martha "wanted nothing more than to live out her life quietly with her husband." Edward J. Larson, *The Return of George Washington* (New York: William Morrow, 2014), 241.

60. GW, letter to Edward Rutledge, May 5, 1789, in *The Writings of George Washington*, vol. 10 (Boston: Little Brown, 1858), 1-2.

61. GW, letter to C. M. Graham, January 9, 1790, in *The Writings of George Washington*, vol. 10 (Boston: Little Brown, 1858), 68.

62. Browne, *First Inauguration*, 153.

63. Ferling, *First of Men*, 480.

64. Rhodenhamel, *George Washington*, 221.

65. GW, letter to David Stuart, June 15, 1790, in *The Writings of George Washington*, vol. 10 (Boston: Little Brown 1858), 101 (also accessed at https://founders.archives.gov/documents/Washington/05-05-02-0334).

66. Rhodenhamel, *George* Washington, 225.

67. Craig Bruce Smith, *American Honor: The Creation of the Nation's Ideals during the Revolutionary Era* (Chapel Hill: University of North Carolina Press, 2018).

68. Smith, *American Honor*, 13.

69. Smith, *American Honor*, 172. Washington served as President-General of the Society of the Cincinnati and continued in that capacity until his death.

70. Smith, *American Honor*, 173.

71. David O. Stewart, *George Washington: The Political Rise of America's Founding Father* (New York: Dutton, 2021), 352.

72. Fleming, *Great Divide*, 127.

73. Stewart, *George Washington*, 352.

74. Because Washington's first term did not technically begin until April 30, 1789, the first day of the next presidential term (designated as March 4 in the year following each presidential election) would actually begin fifty-seven days shy of a full four-year term.

75. The number of justices on the Supreme Court changed six times before settling at the present total of nine in 1869.

76. GW, letter to G. Morris, October 13, 1789, accessed at https://founders.archives.gov/documents/Washington/05-04-02-0125

77. Rhodenhamel, *George Washington*, 261.

78. Burns and Dunn, *George Washington*, 94.

79. Patricia Brady, *Martha Washington: An American Life* (New York: Viking, 2005), 195.

80. Rasmussen, *Fears of a Setting Sun*, 28.

81. Rasmussen, *Fears of a Setting Sun*, 30.

82. David S. Heidler and Jeanne T. Heidler, *Washington's Circle: The Creation of the President* (New York: Random House, 2015), 243-244.

83. Rhodenhamel, *George Washington* 259-260.

84. Stewart, *George Washington*, 352.

85. TJ, letter to GW, May 23, 1792, in *The Writings of George Washington*, vol. 10 (Boston: Little Brown & Co., 1858), 508; See also Fleming, *Great Divide*, 128.

86. Stewart, *George Washington*, 352.

87. Cunningham, *The Presidency of James Monroe* (Lawrence: University Press of Kansas, 1996), 103.

88. Rasmussen, *Fears of a Setting Sun*, 29.

89. Fleming, *Great Divide*, 126.

90. GW, letter to Henry Lee, January 20, 1793, in *The Writings of George Washington*, vol. 10 (Boston: Little Brown, 1858), 312–313.

CHAPTER 2: DECISION (1793–1797)

1. By far the longest inaugural day address (8,445 words) was delivered by William Henry Harrison, who served just thirty-one days as president before succumbing to pneumonia. It was the shortest stint of any American president who formally assumed the office. See https://www.statista.com/statistics/243686/length-of-inaugural-addresses-of-us-presidents/.

2. The president delivered his address that day prior to being administered the oath of office by Associate Justice William Cushing of the United States Supreme Court.

3. John Ferling, *The Ascent of George Washington: The Hidden Political Genius of an American Icon* (New York: Bloomsbury, 2009), 347–348.

4. In what was later termed "the Fauchet scandal," Secretary of State Randolph drew Washington's ire when he exposed the substance of confidential inner cabinet debates to French officials (including French minister Joseph Fauchet). Randolph then made things worse by openly expressing his opinion to those same French officials that the United States had been acting in a hostile way toward their country. The British navy intercepted Randolph's correspondence and turned it over the president, which in turn led to Randolph's resignation.

5. Rhodenhamel, *George Washington*, 286.

6. Only twenty men were arrested, as the rebels departed before Washington's army arrived.

7. John E. Ferling, *Apostles of Revolution: Jefferson, Paine, Monroe, and the Struggle Against the Old Order in America and Europe* (New York: Bloomsbury, 2018), 304

8. Because Great Britain had trouble maintaining enough manpower to meet its military needs, the Royal Navy drafted American soldiers on merchant ships, forcing them to help British soldiers to fight against France. This practice had been highlighted as one of the twenty-seven colonial grievances listed in the Declaration of Independence.

9. GW, letter to Edmund Randolph, July 29, 1795, in *The Writings of George Washington*, volume 11 (Boston: Little Brown, 1858), 47.

10. John E. Ferling, *The First of Men: A Life of George Washington* (New York: Oxford University Press, 1988), 481.

11. Stewart, *George Washington*, 388.

12. Ferling, *Apostles of Revolution*, 30.

13. Coe, *You Never Forget Your First*, 167.

14. Gary Wills, *Cincinnatus: George Washington and the Enlightenment* (New York: Doubleday, 1984), 90.

15. Randall, *George Washington*, 491.

16. Coe, *You Never Forget Your First*, 174.

17. Ferling, *First of Men*, 465.

18. Horn, *Washington's End*, 9.

19. Stewart, *George Washington*, 388.

20. Rhodenhamel, *George Washington*, 259–260.

21. Fleming, *The Great Divide*, 230–231.

22. Rhodenhamel, *George Washington*, 271.

23. Randall, *George Washington*, 491.

24. GW, letter to Edmund Pendleton, January 22, 1795, in *The Writings of George Washington*, vol. 11 (Boston: Little Brown, 1858), 10–11.

25. Horn, *Washington's End*, 4.

26. Miriam Anne Bourne, *First Family*, 171.

27. Coe, *You Never Forget Your First*, 172.

28. GW letter to Thomas Jefferson, July 6, 1796, in *The Writings of George Washington*, vol. 11(Boston: Little Brown., 1858), 137–139.

29. Stewart, *George Washington*, 389.

30. Coe, *You Never Forget Your First*, 173.

31. Fleming, *Great Divide*, 233.

32. Stewart, *George Washington*, 392.

33. Rasmussen, *Fears of a Setting Sun*, 46.

34. Coe, *You Never Forget Your First*, 173.

35. Heidler and Heidler, *Washington's Circle*, 392.

36. Ellis, *His Excellency*, 234.

37. Rasmussen, *Fears of a Setting Sun*, 46.

38. Ferling, *First of Men*, 466.

39. Originally titled "The Address of Gen. Washington to the People of America on His Declining the Presidency of the United States," the letter would later become known as Washington's "Farewell Address to the nation." It was first published in the *American Daily Advertiser*.

40. More than two centuries later, the musical *Hamilton* did a famous send-up of King George's reaction to John Adams's election as the second president of the United States: "John Adams? I know him. That can't be. That's that little guy who spoke to me all those years ago. What was it, eighty-five? That poor man, they're going to eat him alive! Next to Washington, they all look small. All alone. Watch them run. They will tear each other into pieces. Jesus Christ, this will be fun!" (See https://hamiltonmusical.fandom.com/wiki/I_Know_Him). King George was referring to his meeting with the newly appointed United States Minister Plenipotentiary to Britain, on June 1, 1785.

41. Ellis, *His Excellency*, 233. Even though Jefferson was unlikely to challenge

his former boss, other Democrat-Republicans associated with Jefferson were willing to challenge Washington in 1796, including Aaron Burr, Samuel Adams and possibly even George Clinton.

42. Brookheiser, *Founding Father*, 101.

43. Ferling, *Ascent of George Washington*, 347.

44. Ferling, *Ascent of George* Washington, 347.

45. Rhodenhamel, *George Washington*, 287.

46. Chernow, *Washington*, 752. Washington told John Jay that all the troubles he had endured were "aggravated by the infirmities of age" and said only a national emergency would postpone his retirement.

47. Rhodenhamel, *George* Washington, 225–226.

48. Heidler and Heidler, *Washington's Circle*, 79.

49. Ellis, *His Excellency*, 275.

50. Wills, *Cincinnatus*, 162.

51. Larson, *Return of George Washington*, 302.

52. Burns and Dunn, *George Washington*, 128.

53. Stewart, *George*, 389.

54. Rhodenhamel, *George Washington*, 290.

55. Burns and Dunn, *George Washington*, 128.

56. Wills, *Cincinnatus*, 88.

57. Ellis, *American Dialogue*, 198.

CHAPTER 3: AFTERMATH (1797–1951)

1. Fleming, *The Great Divide*, 274.

2. The Federalist Party fielded its last presidential candidate, Rufus King, in 1816. King won just three of 19 states and barely 31 percent of the popular vote. After President Adams's defeat in 1800, the only Federalist to top even 40 percent of the vote was Dewitt Clinton, whose affiliation with the Democrat-Republicans in New York State both before and after the election went a long way to explaining how he secured 47.6 percent of the popular vote.

3. Korzi, *Presidential Term Limits*, 48.

4. Jon Meacham, *Thomas Jefferson: The Art of Power* (New York: Random House, 2012), 408–409.

5. Thomas Jefferson, letter to John Taylor, 1/6/1805.

6. According to the Pulitzer-winning biographer Dumas Malone, Jefferson "had every intention of following Washington's example," as he regarded Washington's precedent as "obligatory," making it "all the more desirable that he himself discountenance the idea of perpetuity in office." Dumas Malone, *Jefferson the President: Second Term 1805–1809* (Charlottesville: University of Virginia Press, 2006), 169.

7. Korzi, *Presidential Term Limits*, 51,

8. Joyce O. Appleby, *Thomas Jefferson* (New York: Henry Holt, 2003), 119.

9. Fleming, *Great Divide*, 358.

10. Christopher Hitchens, *Thomas Jefferson: Author of America* (New York: HarperCollins, 2005), 166.

11. Malone, *Jefferson*, 578.

12. Korzi, *Presidential Term Limits*, 41

13. Cronin, "Presidential Terms," 77.

14. Malone, *Jefferson*, 548, 551; Fleming, *Great Divide*, 36.

15. After Madison was elected, Congress quickly replaced the Embargo Act with the far more diluted Non-Intercourse Act of 1809.

16. Noah Feldman, *The Three Lives of James Madison* (New York: Random House, 2017), 500.

17. Chernow, *Washington*, 593–594.

18. Feldman, *Three Lives*, 616.

19. Article by George Rothwell Brown, quoted in the extension of Remarks of Hon. Albert J. Engel of Michigan, "The Third-Term Issue," *Congressional Record: Proceedings and Debates of the 76th Congress, Second Session*, March 25, 1940 (Appendix), 1625.

20. Cunningham, *The Presidency of James Monroe*, 167.

21. Korzi, *Presidential Term Limits*, 52.

22. *Moves to Limit the Term, 1787-1947*, 26 Congressional Digest 14, 15 (1947) (summarizing political initiatives to limit "the Presidential tenure of office" from 1787 to 1947).

23. Ulysses S. Grant, State of the Union Address, submitted to the Senate and the House of Represetatives, December 5, 1876.

24. Apparently, an aide to the ex-president (Adam Badeau) commented that Grant had become "extremely anxious to receive the nomination" and did not think that there was any chance of failure.

25. Chernow, *Grant*, 901.

26. Kenneth Ackerman, *Dark Horse: The Surprise Election and Political Murder of President James A. Garfield*. (New York: Carroll & Graf, 2003), 48.

27. Chernow, *Grant*, 899.

28. Chernow, *Grant*, 900.

29. John Y. Simon, "Ulysses Grant," in *The Presidents: A Reference History*, seventh edition (2002), ed. Henry Graff, 253.

30. Richard E. Welch, Jr., *The Presidencies of Grover Cleveland* (Lawrence: University Press of Kansas, 1988), 210

31. Kendrick Clements, *The Presidency of Woodrow Wilson* (Lawrence: University Press of Kansas, 1992), 203.

32. Clements, *The Presidency of Woodrow Wilson*, 203.

33. Werling, Charles J., "The Nomination of James M. Cox: The Democratic Convention of 1920" (1965). Master's Thesis. 2046. https://ecommons.luc.edu/luc_theses/2046, 94.

34. Robert H. Ferrell, *The Presidency of Calvin Coolidge* (Lawrence: University Press of Kansas, 1998), 197.

35. Robert Sobel, *Coolidge: An American Enigma* (Washington DC: Regnery, 1998), 371–372.

36. Sobel, *Coolidge*, 368.

37. When Cordell Hull's wife told the President that her husband did not like to make speeches, the president reportedly replied: "well, tell him he had better get used to it . . . he'll have a lot of it to do soon." Jean Edward Smith, *FDR* (New York: Random House, 2007), 443.

38. Smith, *FDR*, 441.

39. Franklin D. Roosevelt, *Radio Address to the Democratic National Convention Accepting the Nomination*, Chicago, Illinois, July 19, 1940.

40. Roosevelt would go on to take a fourth oath of office on January 20, 1945. For his part, Willkie suffered over a dozen heart attacks during Roosevelt's third term and died on October 8, 1944.

41. Lydia Saad, "Gallup Vault: War Stirred Support for Roosevelt's Third Term," *Gallup Website*, June 24, 2016 (accessed at https://news.gallup.com/vault /193148/gallup-vault-war-stirred-support-roosevelt-third-term.aspx)

42. Smith, *FDR*, 457.

43. Smith, *FDR*, 475.

44. Smith, *FDR*, 475.

45. American Presidency Project, "President Job Approval Ratings for Harry S. Truman," https://www.presidency.ucsb.edu/statistics/data/presidential-job-approval.

CONCLUSION: LOOKING BACK AND LOOKING AHEAD

1. Chris Cilliza, "Believe It or Not, Donald Trump Says He Should Get a Third Term," *CNN.com*, August 18, 2020, https://www.cnn.com/2020/08/18/politics /donald-trump-third-term-2024/index.html. President Trump made similar comments live and via Twitter many times between 2017 and 2020. In the spring of 2018, while addressing a crowd of donors during an event at his Florida estate, Trump spoke about the recent amendment of China's constitution to remove presidential term limits, allowing President Xi Jinping to serve in that office indefinitely. About Xi, Trump said: "He's now president for life, president for life. And he's great. . . . And look, he was able to do that. I think it's great. Maybe we'll have to give that a shot someday." David Shepardson, "Trump Praises Chinese President Extending Tenure 'for Life,'" *Reuters*, Mar. 3, 2018, https://www.reuters .com/article/us-trump-china/trump-praises-chinese-president-extending-tenure -for-life-idUSKCN1GG015.

2. Bertrand Russell, *Power: A New Social Analysis* (1938; repr. New York: Routledge, 2004).

3. Thomas Jefferson, reply to the Legislature of Vermont, 1807, in Lipscomb and Bergh, eds., *The Writings of Thomas Jefferson, Memorial Edition*, vol. 16 (Washington DC. 1903–04), 293.

BIBLIOGRAPHIC ESSAY

There exists a vast literature of excellent books, articles, and scholarly works on George Washington. Given that his decision to leave the presidency after two terms followed so naturally from the life he lived and the lessons he culled from that life, full biographies of Washington were a natural place to begin when doing research on how the two-term precedent was first established.

Chronologically speaking, Washington Irving's five-volume biography of the first president—he completed *The Life of George Washington* only eight months before he died of a heart attack in 1859—was the first to go beyond fawning hagiography. It was also the first biography to include a comprehensive account of Washington's personal life based on his own letters and diaries. Despite generally poor editing and inconsistent coverage, true George Washington aficionados will want to take the plunge into Irving's work. In the twentieth century, Douglas Southall Freeman wrote perhaps the most comprehensive and authoritative biography of Washington produced up to that time. His seven-volume biography (published intermittently from 1948 through 1957) earned him a Pulitzer Prize (albeit posthumously, in 1958). While Freeman's research is methodical and painstaking, large parts of the story are told primarily from Washington's own viewpoint, causing it to miss some important perspectives as a result. James Thomas Flexner's *Washington: The Indispensable Man* (Boston: Little, Brown & Co, 1994) offers a single volume distillation of his Pulitzer-prize winning, four-volume series that was released between 1965 and 1972. Flexner focuses on Washington as a fallible human being, providing a necessary counterpoint to Freeman's work and many of the positive accounts that preceded him.

A number of excellent Washington biographies have also appeared in recent decades. For readers who seek a comprehensive one-volume biography of the first president, one cannot find a better work than Ron Chernow's Pulitzer Prize–winning *Washington: A Life* (New York: Penguin, 2010). Time and time again, I would discover some little-known fact about Washington from another source, and then race over to Chernow's biography to get his authoritative (and often elegant) take on that same matter. Of course, if a 904-page tome is simply too daunting, one can more quickly consume *His Excellency: George Washington* (New York: Vintage, 2004) by Joseph Ellis, which is nearly as impressive, and yet comes in at 352 pages. The Ellis and Chernow biographies stand out as among the best in this well-trodden genre.

In addition, there are numerous other one-volume biographies which—while never reaching the heights of Ellis's and Chernow's efforts—still provide quite valuable treatments of Washington's life as a whole. Among the best of these were Willard Sterne Randall's *George Washington: A Life* (New York: Henry Holt, 1997); Richard Brookhiser's *George Washington: Founding Father* (New York: Free Press, 1996); John Rhodehamel's *George Washington: The Wonder of the Age* (New

Haven: Yale University Press, 2017); and John E. Ferling's *The First of Men: A Life of George Washington* (New York: Oxford University Press, 1988). More than two decades later, Ferling wrote yet another book about Washington that dug deeper into his political genius without offering the full biographic treatment in his first effort (John Ferling, *The Ascent of George Washington* [New York: Bloomsbury, 2009]. While this later work does not explore Washington's family or personal relationships as a complete biography would, it starts during his childhood and covers his military and political careers in such detail that it accomplishes much of a biographer's goals in any event.

Though Washington's background as a planter and military hero laid the groundwork for his ultimate decision to abandon the presidency, the lead-up to the 1787 Constitutional Convention and Washington's role in helping to design the chief executive under the new constitution are more directly connected to Washington's later thinking on the issue. The last decade has seen a resurgence of interest in Washington's understated but influential role during these events. Few books cover this period better than Edward Larson's *The Return of George Washington: 1783–1789* (New York: HarperCollins, 2014). Other important works include Stephen Howard Browne's *The First Inauguration: George Washington and the Invention of the Republic* (University Park: Pennsylvania State University State Press, 2020); Harlow Giles Unger's *Mr. President: George Washington and the Making of the Nation's Highest Office* (Boston: De Capo, 2013) and David S. Heidler and Jeanne T. Heidler, *Washington's Circle: The Creation of the President* (New York: Random House, 2015).

On George Washington's second term in particular, when his key decisions about retirement took their final shape, see John Avalon, *Washington's Farewell: The Founding Father's Warning to Future Generations* (New York: Simon & Schuster, 2017). As for his oft-forgotten post-presidency, I learned much from Jonathan Horn's *Washington's End: The Final Years and Forgotten Struggle* (New York: Simon & Schuster, 2020). Washington is one of a handful of American presidents whose legacy alone offers a fruitful area of study. Several decades ago, Barry Schwartz took up this challenge in *George Washington: The Making of an American Symbol* (New York: Free Press, 1987). A more recent and easy-to-read contribution to this subject is Francois Furstenberg's *In the Name of the Father: Washington's Legacy, Slavery, and the Making of a Nation* (New York: Penguin Press, 2006). And for those interested in a more light-hearted tour of the way Washington has been misremembered by so many, see Alexis Coe, *You Never Forget Your First* (New York: Viking Press, 2020).

In doing this research, I was amazed to find so few treatments of the Roman legend Lucius Quinctius Cincinnatus, whose own life story so influenced Washington and his contemporaries. Naturally, his name comes up in more general works about ancient Rome, but rarely have historians plowed deeply into the recorded life of Cincinnatus. One notable exception is Michael J. Hillyard's *Cincinnatus and the Citizen-Servant Ideal* (New York: Xlibris, 2001). Additionally, the political philosopher and historian Garry Wills closely examined the connections between Cincinnatus and Washington in *Cincinnatus: George Washington and The Enlightenment* (New York: Doubleday, 1984).

By contrast, the literature on the founding fathers and Washington's place as a thinker within that pantheon is enormous. Though this book never intended to offer a comprehensive account of the role played by other founding fathers in establishing a new constitution, three recent works stand out for their compelling analysis of Washington's role vis-à -vis the others: John Ferling's *Apostles of Revolution* (New York: Bloomsbury, 2018) and Thomas Fleming's *The Great Divide* (Boston: De Capo, 2015) discuss how and why Washington differed so much from Thomas Jefferson in particular in his approach to former revolutionaries who turned partisan and the establishment of the federal government under the new Constitution. Additionally, Dennis C. Rasmussen's thought-provoking *Fears of a Setting Sun: The Disillusionment of America's Founders* (Princeton: Princeton University Press, 2021) tells the story of the Founders' genuine fears about the American experiment, and it outlines the frustrations and concerns that drove their decision making throughout this period. Joseph Ellis's *American Dialogue: The Founders and Us* (New York: Alfred Knopf, 2018) is also a valuable read on this important topic.

When it comes to the history of presidential term limits more generally, the most authoritative works can be found primarily in journals (for academics or laypersons) and not in book-length manuscripts. The one notable exception—and thus a crucial source of information for this book—is Michael J. Korzi's *Presidential Term Limits in American History: Power, Principles, and Politics* (College Station: Texas A & M University Press, 2011). As I argue in Chapter 3, Korzi tends to give a bit too much credit to Jefferson for embedding the two-term tradition into our political culture. On the other hand, Korzi offers excellent historical perspective on presidential term limits. My argument was greatly improved by the fact that I was forced to meet Korzi's argument on his own terms.

Meanwhile, the best journal article by far on this subject was Bruce Peabody and Scott Gant, "The Twice and Future President: Constitutional Interstices and the Twenty-Second Amendment," *Minnesota Law Review* 83 (1999), pp. 565–635. Numerous other articles also proved invaluable, including David A. Crockett, "'An Excess of Refinement': Lame Duck Presidents in Constitutional and Historical Context," *Presidential Studies Quarterly* 38, no. 4 (December 2008), pp. 707–721; Stephen W. Stathis, "The Twenty-Second Amendment: A Practical Remedy or Partisan Maneuver?" *Constitutional Commentary* 7 (1990), pp. 61–88; Harry A. Bailey, Jr., "Presidential Tenure and the Two-Term Tradition," *Publius* 2, no. 2 (Autumn 1972), pp. 95–106; and John William Perrin, "Presidential Tenure and Eligibility," *Political Science Quarterly* 29, no. 3 (September 1914), pp. 423–27. I also benefited from a Congressional Research Service report entitled "Presidential Terms and Tenure: Perspectives and Proposal for Change," Report No. R40864 (updated April 15, 2019).

As one might expect, there are many scholarly works that go in-depth on the individual presidents who faced the dilemma of whether or not to buck Washington's example and run for a third term. On Jefferson: Dumas Malone, *Jefferson the President: 2nd Term*, vol. 5 (Charlottesville: University of Virginia Press, 2006); Jon Meacham, *Thomas Jefferson: The Art of Power* (New York: Random House, 2006); and Joseph Ellis, *American Sphinx: The Character of Thomas Jefferson* (New York: Vintage, 1998). On Madison: Richard Brookhiser, *James Madison* (New York: Basic, 2011) and Noah Feldman, *The Three Lives of James Madison: Genius, Partisan, President* (New York: Random House, 2017). On James Monroe: Harlow Unger, *The Last Founding Father: James Monroe* (Boston: Da Capo, 2010); On Andrew Jackson: Robert Remini, *The Life of Andrew Jackson* (New York: Harper, 2010); Jon Meacham, *American Lion: Andrew Jackson in the White House* (New York: Random House, 2009); and H. W. Brands, *Andrew Jackson: His Life and Times* (New York: Anchor, 2006). On Ulysses Grant: Jean Edward Smith, *Grant* (New York: Simon & Schuster, 2002); William McFeely, *Grant: A Biography* (New York: W. W. Norton, 2002); and Ron Chernow, *Grant* (New York: Penguin Press, 2017); On Theodore Roosevelt: H. W. Brands, *TR: The Last Romantic* (New York: Basic, 1998); Edmund Morris, *Theodore Rex* (New York: Random House, 2002); Kathleen Dalton, *Theodore Roosevelt: A Strenuous Life* (New York: Vintage, 2004). On Woodrow Wilson: A. Scott Berg, *Wilson* (New York: G. P. Putnam's Sons, 2013) and John Milton, Cooper, Jr., *Woodrow Wilson: A Biography* (New York: Vintage Books, 2011); On Calvin Coolidge: Donald McCoy, *Calvin Coolidge: The Quiet President* (New York: American Political Biography Press, 2000) and Robert Sobel, *Coolidge: An American Enigma* (New York: Regnery, 2000). And on Franklin Delano Roosevelt: Jean Edward Smith, *FDR* (New York: Random House, 2008); H. W. Brands, *Traitor to his Class: The Privileged Life and Radical Presidency of FDR* (New York: Anchor, 2009); and Conrad Black, *FDR: Champion of Freedom* (New York: Public Affairs, 2003).

Finally, for this project I was transported most effectively into the 1790s whenever I examined the words of George Washington himself. In 1833, George Washington's nephew, Bushrod Washington, provided the American historian Jared Sparks with access to the vast majority of George Washington's correspondence and writings. After publishing his own two-volume biography of Washington based on those sources, Sparks subsequently produced a twelve-volume series (which he published between 1833 and 1837) that featured all of Washington's writings. I went back to the final three volumes of the set on many occasions, finding rich new material in each instance. For those who prefer to do their work by referring to a single volume, much of this material is duplicated in *George Washington: Selected Writings* (New York: Library of America Classics, 2011) and in *George Washington: Writings*, edited by John Rhodenhamel (Library of America, 1997).

INDEX